The Way of Life

The writings attributed to Lao Tzu, and called *Tao Té Ching*, are second only to Confucianism in their influence on and importance to China through the ages. Consisting of eighty-one brief poems, they compose the cherished beliefs of Taoism, which is devoted to a denial of selfishness and self-seeking and to a mystical union with the ultimate.

Tao Té Ching (pronounced *Dow Dŭh Jing*) is the way of life defined by many ancient sages who lived in China centuries ago. There was one man, Lao Tzu, called the Old One, who practiced "the way." But there were other religious thinkers who lived in remote valleys of China and who contributed further ideas and wisdom to it. Altogether, *Tao Té Ching* expresses a way of life at once a mystic religion and a philosophy advocating simplicity, frugality, and the joys of living close to the soil.

R. B. Blakney, past president of Olivet College, former missionary and teacher in China, and author of many volumes on Eastern religions, made this splendid translation of a great gem of Chinese religion and provided an illuminating interpretative commentary.

Richard John Lynn is Professor Emeritus of Chinese Thought and Literature, Department of East Asian Studies, University of Toronto, Canada. His publications include books on the Yuan-era poet *Kuan Yün-shih*, *Chinese Literature: A Draft Bibliography in Western European Languages*, *Guide to Chinese Poetry and Drama*, *The Classic of Changes: A New Translation of the I Ching as Interpreted by Wang Bi*, *The Classic of the Way and Virtue: A New Translation of the Tao-te ching of Laozi as Interpreted by Wang Bi*. He is the editor of James J. Y. Liu's *Language—Paradox—Poetics: A Chinese Perspective*.

TAO TÉ CHING

Translated and with an Introduction by
R. B. Blakney

With a New Afterword by
Richard John Lynn

Previously published as
The Way of Life

SIGNET CLASSICS

SIGNET CLASSICS
Published by New American Library, a division of
Penguin Group (USA) Inc., 375 Hudson Street,
New York, New York 10014, USA
Penguin Group (Canada), 90 Eglinton Avenue East, Suite 700, Toronto,
Ontario M4P 2Y3, Canada (a division of Pearson Penguin Canada Inc.)
Penguin Books Ltd., 80 Strand, London WC2R 0RL, England
Penguin Ireland, 25 St. Stephen's Green, Dublin 2,
Ireland (a division of Penguin Books Ltd.)
Penguin Group (Australia), 250 Camberwell Road, Camberwell, Victoria
3124, Australia (a division of Pearson Australia Group Pty. Ltd.)
Penguin Books India Pvt. Ltd., 11 Community Centre, Panchsheel Park,
New Delhi - 110 017, India
Penguin Group (NZ), cnr Airborne and Rosedale Roads, Albany,
Auckland 1310, New Zealand (a division of Pearson New Zealand Ltd.)
Penguin Books (South Africa) (Pty.) Ltd., 24 Sturdee Avenue,
Rosebank, Johannesburg 2196, South Africa

Penguin Books Ltd., Registered Offices:
80 Strand, London WC2R 0RL, England

Published by Signet Classics, an imprint of New American Library, a division
of Penguin Group (USA) Inc. Previously published in Signet Classics and
Mentor editions as *The Way of Life*.

First Signet Classics Printing (*Tao Té Ching*), January 2007
10 9 8 7 6 5 4 3

Copyright © Robert B. Blakney, 1955
Copyright © renewed Charles Philip Blakney, 1983
Afterword copyright © Richard John Lynn, 2007
All rights reserved

Contents

5

Preface

Thirty years ago in Foochow, China's great contribution to the literature of mysticism began to fascinate me; and the urge to read it with the care required for a translation became strong. It has remained strong through the years, even though other work has denied it satisfaction. I suspect that nearly every foreigner in China who has taken the trouble to study this collection of mystical poems has felt the same way: so many translations of it have appeared. For one reason or another each translation, in its turn, fails fully to satisfy one who knows the original, and at length, one tries his own hand at it. Will he, in his turn, satisfy? Probably not; but he may add his share to the ultimate understanding of one of the world's truly distinguished religious works.

Fortunately, the translation of the *Tao Té Ching* is not now as difficult as it was thirty years ago. Recent scholarship has thrown strong light on many passages that would otherwise be dark or dim. There are still cloud banks here and there in the text, but with care, it is possible to get through them reasonably well. The *Tao Té Ching* was by no means written in a vacuum, and increased knowledge of contemporary thought and conditions helps both translator and reader to understand it better. Acquaintance with the ways of mystics of other lands and times is also useful. The Chinese mystics were original and to the point in their writing, but their point was identical with that of the great mystics elsewhere.

"The Way of Life," chosen as the English title of this translation, is partly arbitrary. Literally, *Tao Té Ching* (pronounced approximately *Dow Dŭh Jing*) means *The Book of the Way and Its Virtue,* but this would make a clumsy and perhaps forbidding adver-

tisement for these poems. "The Way of Life" is neater
and will not be too misleading if it is understood that
"life" was, to these mystics, a virtue imparted by the
Way to all creation and a virtue from which nothing
was wholly exempt.

Assuming then that the English title thus chosen
will prove attractive, it has seemed to me better to
use the widely familiar Chinese title in the Introduction and the text proper. Most readers find it easy to
become addicted to these three compact words, even
though at first they sound and look strange. They have
the virtue for us of allowing the mystics themselves to
define and develop their theme, undistracted by the
connotations of alien words.

I cannot pretend to see the world as Chinese of the
third to the sixth centuries before Christ saw it, and I
do not believe that any amount of scientific sifting of
the facts would enable a person of this century to do
so. There will always remain a semantic gulf between
them and us, one that must be bridged by adding insight and imagination to considered evidence. If then
the reader of a translation of the *Tao Té Ching* asks,
"Is this really what they meant?", the translator can
only reply humbly, "To the best of my knowledge,
yes." But he will always be uncertain to some degree,
since the original authors are unavailable to check his
work. In this respect, the translation of recent or contemporary works is much surer.

It is my belief that a finished translation should be
free of all traces of the original language, especially
when they mar English diction. If parts of the original
are obdurately obscure, it is better, it seems to me, to
omit them rather than to carry the obscurity over into
English. Of course, it is possible, as the great Jacobean
translators of the Bible demonstrated, to write the
original up, and make it appear to rise higher than its
source. But if that happens, it had better be by pure
accident. The translator is, I believe, obligated to write
the original neither up nor down.

The translated excerpts from *The Book of Odes* are

based on the excellent Chinese text edited by Bernhard Karlgren and published by the Museum of Far Eastern Antiquities, Stockholm, 1950.

For the translations of the citations from *The Book of Lord Shang,* I am indebted to the careful work of J. J. Duyvendak (London: Probsthain, 1928). Otherwise, the translations are my own. I acknowledge gratefully that it has by no means been necessary to start from scratch: I have seen and studied the results of other careful workmen in the field.

I have borrowed ideas and sometimes the meat of comment from the chapter on mysticism in Dr. W. E. Hocking's *Types of Philosophy.* For these helps, I am deeply grateful, as I am to the many other friends and writers who, through the years, have contributed unwittingly to this translation. At the proper place I have acknowledged the contribution of my long-time friend and colleague Dr. Roderick Scott. I also owe a special debt to Professor Shao-Chang Lee, of Michigan State College, for reading and commenting on my manuscript and for the loan of a valuable text: *Lao Chieh Lao.* To Mrs. Roland Lawler, née *Ku Chüan Ying,* thanks are due for the text of Poem 32 in Chinese and for designing most of the Chinese words discussed in the Introduction.

—R. B. Blakney

What was desired was that through this man the way in which God works should be made manifest. (John 9:3)

E. V. RIEU, trans.

Introduction

Somewhat more than a millennium before Christ, a people known as the Shang or Yin lived along the Yellow River in north central China. Of their origin and history very little is known certainly, except that their civilization was relatively old and rich, and finally effete. They left abundant evidence of great technical skill in casting bronze, of their artistry in pottery and of their ingenuity in the creation of written words which are the direct ancestors of modern Chinese characters. From inscriptions on bone and bronze, the names of some of their kings are known and also the nature of their divination.

About 1100 B.C., they were conquered by a neighboring people, known as the Chou, for whom the Chou dynasty, the longest in Chinese history, is named. The fame of the Chou rests chiefly on the development of an extensive written literature and on the fresh, original thinking of philosophers and investigators of first rank: Confucius, Mencius, Chuang Chou, and the writers of the poems* in the *Tao Té Ching,* not to mention others, less decisive, but not less able in their way.

This burst of intellectual effort, which subsequently gave the Chinese people matter for thought and commentaries over two and one-half millenniums, began in the sixth century B.C. with Confucius (551–479). It was preceded by five dim centuries under Chou kings, who seem to have been able and vigorous at first, but who deteriorated in character and ability as their prosperity grew.

*Some scholars prefer to call the "poems" of the *Tao Té Ching* chapters.

15

Book of Odes

There are archeological remains of the period which tell us much, but the human detail has to be gleaned from books whose early history and meaning are often unclear. One of these, and perhaps the more important, is an anthology known as the *Book of Odes,* said to have been edited by Confucius himself. Some of the poems came from Shang times, some are love songs of delicacy and feeling, and some comment on the vicissitudes of Chou government and politics and the concomitant elation or depression of the people.

Certainly the *Book of Odes* furnished both Confucius and the poets of the *Tao Té Ching* with basic food for thought. It made reflection possible. No event of their time, whether happy or unhappy, was isolated, as it must have been before there was written literature. They had before them, in rather elegant form, the reactions of literate men of their own kind to similar events in preceding centuries. They could make comparisons and draw conclusions, which were formed in the process of long debates and which have come down to us in at least foreshortened form. The Chou philosophers had a very considerable body of written tradition on which to draw.

Confucius not only quoted the *Odes* frequently but recommended them to his students: "My little ones, why don't you study the *Odes*? Poetry will exalt you, make you observant, enable you to mix with others, provide an outlet for your vexations; you learn from it immediately to serve your parents and ultimately to serve your prince. It also provides wide acquaintance with the names of birds, beasts, and plants." (*Analects* XVII:9.)

Here, for example, is a series of passages from the *Odes,* which must have given the early Chou thinkers pause:

August indeed is God* on high;
Fearful too when he draws near;
When he surveyed the world,
Sought peace for all the folk,
In Hsia and Shang, these two,
He found bad government . . .
God took them then in hand,
Hating their lavish life,
And turned his gaze toward the west
And gave their land to Chou. (241:1)

In the succession of Chou,
Each generation produced
A king who was wise and who knew.
In heaven now are three;
And the king in the capital
Is fitly their counterpart. (243:1)

Because the king remained
Inerrant in virtue,
The nations surrounding
Were given to him. (236:3)

But as time went on, the kings weakened; the government devolved upon eunuchs and timeservers; rapacious tyranny developed, and banditry and general disorder became common:

The people are tired to death
They should have a little peace;
Be kind to this central realm
So the others too may rest. (253:1)

Then, for full measure, there were natural calamities:

Now God is sending
Vast famines and pestilence;

*For "God" as a translation of *T'ien* see page 47.

Death and disorder abound.
The talk of the people is bad
Since no one assuages their grief. (191:2)

The great God is unjust
So to oppress us with calamity!
The great God is unkind
To send down such offense! (191:5)

Great pitiless God!
Will disorders never cease?
Every month they grow
And people have no peace. (191:6)

The testimony of the *Odes* is fairly obvious. Somewhat before the midpoint of the Chou dynasty, there was revolt against the gods, whether conceived as the illustrious dead (*Kuei, Shen*), or the high God (*Shang Ti*), or as vast Heaven (*Hao Tien*). It was not that the folk were exceptionally moral or immoral, for such considerations were not established, except perhaps in isolated individuals; but the folk *were* religious. The required rites, propitiating the unseen powers or offering tribute to them, were generally performed as immemorial custom dictated. The unseen world had no grounds for complaint, and yet, evil after evil descended from above until the folk could no longer bear their suffering. The wrong they felt was rudimentary but powerful and they attributed it variously to those powers from which all human fate proceeded.

Occasionally, some more sensitive person, in sad disgust, would go off alone to brood over his wrongs, the wickedness and inhumanity of the king's court, the growing poverty and disorder, or the famines and plagues by which heaven was increased at the expense of earth. Perhaps some of the odes were the fruit of the brooding of these recluses. It is hard to imagine such poems of protest being written within reach of the king. Occasionally one of them signed his work: "Chia-fu made this poem to explore the king's wickedness. If you would but change your heart, the nations might be fed!" (*Ibid.,* 191:10.)

Chia-fu and his kind were the articulate underground. They uttered and perhaps wrote these occasional poetic protests. Their oral efforts must have found wide circulation, but their reading public was probably concentrated close to the king's court!

It is the sick who create physicians, men who recognize the systematic nature of sickness and are prepared to offer systematic cures. Toward the end of the sixth century, we may assume that the *Odes* had been collected and studied sufficiently to suggest the systematic nature of the evils that afflicted the loose collection of feudal states into which the Chou empire had disintegrated. Two schools of physicians appeared with systematic cures. One of them was dramatized in the person of Confucius, who proposed the moral cure for the evils of society. The other originated more obscurely, perhaps among the recluses brooding in the mountain valleys and among whom the *Tao Té Ching* first took form. These offered mysticism.

Confucius

It is no accident that China's great moral innovator was a gregarious man who haunted capital cities, accompanied by disciples, pleading for a chance to set things right. Nor is it an accident that an important and original expression of the great mysticism of all time was conceived in some of China's valleys. The purely moral proposal is most probable where people press together and life requires general agreement on its conduct. The mystic view becomes probable where individuals confront the universe alone. In China, the masses of people have always been pressed together. So they are moral; and Confucius has been their representative man. Mysticism still survives in China but rather on the periphery of life, where there is room.

Dr. W. E. Hocking thinks that Confucius and the mystics shared a dominant, common trait: metaphysical reticence. As far as Confucius is concerned, he was quite right: "Tzu Kung said, our Master's views on culture and refinement are for all to hear but what he has to say about the nature of man and the ways of God no one ever hears." (*Analects* V:12.)

The great Chinese felt that he had been divinely appointed to teach moral excellence and he would not say more than he knew. "God begot the virtue in me." It was not his own.

The mystics, however, were not reticent. Theirs was a problem of communication. They had discovered, they said, a unique Something for which there was no word or name (25*). It did not belong to the world in which language is born. The world was its by-product and nothing could exist without it. What was more immediate, there could be no good government or well-being for man apart from it. Still, it was *sui generis,* of its own kind.

Their only recourse was to borrow a sign for it (25) and give that sign a meaning it never had before. For a sign they chose a word already old and familiar, one that Confucius had used in a more limited sense. The word was Tao, the Way, but only those who shared their discovery at firsthand could know what they meant by it. Confucius, for example, could not. "It is of no use," he said, "to confer with those of a different Way." (*Analects* XV:39.)

It would be better to say that Confucius and the mystics shared a common skepticism about the Way as people generally understood it. It was said to be the Way of the congregation of heaven to indicate its pleasure or displeasure with the ways of men by signs and omens, and to punish or reward them by sending down bad or good times. It was therefore the Way of men to humor the heavenly host with sacrifices and rites, and to keep it informed, through prayers, of what went on. In the

*The numerals in parentheses throughout this manuscript refer to individual poems in the *Tao Té Ching* unless otherwise identified.

face of the colossal evils that had befallen the Chou, a new conception of the Way was required if the nation was to survive. The thinkers of Chou were occupied with this problem until the "First Emperor," in 221 B.C., solved the problem by abolishing it.

The Confucian Way was to be punctilious about the rites and sacrifices but for new reasons. The Master himself seems to have discarded the idea that ritual acts could be the cause of certain effects desired by men: "When the Master was very ill, Tzu Lu requested that prayers be offered. 'Is that done?' the Master asked. 'It is,' Tzu Lu replied. 'The litany says, "Prayers have been offered for you to both earth and sky spirits." ' The Master said, 'My prayers have been offered long since.' " (*Analects* VII:34.) His meaning was that his life had been his prayer. If God was not moved by that, ritual prayers would add nothing. In its way, this was revolutionary.

Ritual was, nevertheless, extremely useful in his eyes. It was the symbol of orderly intercourse between man and God; it could easily be extended to control the relations between man and man when interpreted as etiquette; and it was not difficult for later Confucianists to extend the term until it embraced all civilization. Confucius himself felt that moral character is the root of civilization. Life ritual, or etiquette, is only the outward and visible sign of inner goodness. There is an orderly humane way to live and that is the chief care of a superior man. Confucius would have agreed cheerfully that "order is heaven's first law."

Preoccupation with the *way* of living led naturally to the elaboration of codes of conduct and deportment (20). Eventually, one who aspired to preferment had to master something like 3,300 rules of conduct; this required an effort so great that there could have been little energy left to consider the moral character denoted by one's deportment. Every life situation had its appropriate attitude and response, and the superior man tended to become merely the superior actor, but hardly a person to save decadent Chou.

Confucius himself seems to have foreseen this flaw in his doctrine. Repeatedly, he had advised the promotion of men of superior capacity to high government posts, but when asked how such men could be recognized, he could only answer, "Promote those you know to be such!" Later he confessed that "there well may be men who are superior but not good." Indeed, this has often been the nemesis of Confucian civilization. When there were government promotions to be made, many of those who aspired to preferment were well versed in gentlemanly deportment and other scholarly matters, but had little else to offer.

Strictly speaking, Confucius was no intellectual. No curiosity tempted him beyond the human realm in any direction. He was not a systematic thinker. His version of Tao was that it was the Way of the Ancients, defined presumably from his own reading of written tradition. Men had moral force or character (*Té*) from which their effectiveness was derived, but he did not speculate on the origin of this all-important essence. He stressed filial piety and illustrated it in his own person, but he probably never made it the stultifying force it became in later Confucianism. He often referred to "heaven" colloquially and as if it meant, in general, what the English word "God" means, but here again he would neither speculate nor analyze. That was not his Way.

His lasting greatness rests on his discovery of the moral nature of man and the massive humanism that developed in China in subsequent centuries as a result of his discovery. In some sense, without ever having exercised significant authority, he was the Moses of China.

But the Moses of China had no Promised Land in view, either in one of the "four directions" or vertically. With his discovery of the moral nature of man, he had lighted a great light. It showed how men might *be* better and *do* better where they were. He offered a prescription for peace and order, and his followers developed it into an elaborate pattern of civilization. Within the pattern, endless refinements were possible and were accomplished. The pattern also offered a long-range security to the Chinese way of life which, if it was not entirely shockproof, was still able to defy an astonishing series of conquests by foreign races. The demise of the Confucian way has often been announced in our time, but the announcements may still prove to be premature.

Perhaps the Confucian way has endured so long because it appealed strongly to the common sense of the Chinese people. The deeper excitements of the spirit, however, have had to be secured otherwise, outside Confucian orthodoxy; and over the centuries the Chinese have found them in Buddhism or Taoism, for example. Individual conformity to the given pattern of life has always been inevitable among the teeming populations of China, but even among these patient people it has never been enough.

Mo Ti

It was not enough in the centuries immediately after Confucius. Philosophers of many shades of doctrine, each with his own excitement, competed for royal favor, gathered disciples and spiritual progeny. There was Mo Ti, born the year Confucius died. Where the great Master had been silent, Mo Ti spoke freely and with evident excitement about the love of God (*T'ien*). "The question now is," he said, "What does God want and what does he hate? God wants men to love and be profitable to each other. . . . You must do what God wants and avoid what he hates. . . ." For Mo Ti and his followers the agnosticism implicit in Confucius' references to God and Man was dispelled, as if by a fresh revelation. Mo Ti's converts began to meet in groups to repeat or chant his words. They acted like people who had been living underground and who suddenly had been led out to stand under the blue sky.

For two centuries, Mo Ti and his followers enjoyed an influence so great as to make them formidable rivals of the Confucianists. Their doctrines of God and all-embracing love seemed, at first, to add a new dimension to the world of men. Logically then, Mo Ti made strenuous attacks on aggressive warfare, the lavish funerals that impoverished people, the extravagance of court life. He left essays against fatalism and even against music, both of which he regarded as diverting people's attention from the strenuous efforts immediately required to save the empire from growing disorder.

At some point, an inevitable criticism had to be met: "Today, knights and princes everywhere say, 'All-embracing love is well enough but it is hard to apply where it counts!' Our Master Mo Tzu replied, 'The world's leaders have no idea of what is for their own profit. . . . Those who love others will be loved in return. Do good to others and others will do good to you. Hate people and be hated by them. Hurt them and they will hurt you. What is hard about that?' " (Mo Ti, chap. 15.) Mo Ti, having made his point about the all-embracing love of God, seems to have dropped it there and made his appeal in terms of human self-interest. Warfare, rites, extravagance, music and funerals, which might have been attacked on principle, were instead weighed like merchandise on the scales and found wanting.

The excitement departed from what might have been a serious intellectual movement and might have overcome or at least supplemented the weaknesses of Confucian orthodoxy. After the Chou era, Mo Ti and his successors were all but forgotten in China until recent times. Their failure, paradoxically, was a failure of intellect. They tried to combine all-embracing love with the principle of self-interest.

Shang Yang and the Legalists

Logically, Mo Ti's successor was one Shang Yang, who died in 338 B.C. Like Mo Ti, he was utilitarian; unlike Mo Ti, he was single-minded and thoroughgoing. His views are preserved, probably at second- or thirdhand, in a work known as the *Book of Lord Shang* (*Shang Chün Shu*). He was China's Machiavelli-in-action. "There is more than one way to govern the world," he said, "and there is no need to imitate antiquity. . . . The means by which a ruler encourages people are office and rank: the means by which a country is made prosperous are agriculture and war. . . . Now if titles follow upon the people's exertion of strength, if rewards follow upon their acquisition of merit and if the prince succeeds in making people believe in this as firmly as they do in the shining of sun and moon, then his army will have no equal. . . . Therefore my teaching is to issue such orders that people, if they are desirous of profit, can attain their aim only by agriculture, and if they want to avoid harm, can escape it only by war." (Duyvendak, trans.)

Advocating detailed laws, enforced by heavy punishments, Shang Yang was the first of a school later to be known as the *Fa Chia,* the Legalists. Under his guiding hand, the semibarbarous state of Ch'in, far to the west, began to be totalitarian in a modern sense. Its area was large and its population sparse. It needed farmers to support its armies and armies to accomplish the ambitions of its king. To the south and east, there were small neighboring states with plenty of excellent farmers. This situation may have suggested to Shang Yang his notable chapter on "The Encouragement of Immigration."

Sometime in the third century B.C., the king of Ch'in began to "encourage" immigration positively, and his armies swarmed over the little lands, finally extinguishing the embers of the Chou empire. In 221, he became the self-styled "First Emperor" of China; and for a brief period, perhaps less than a generation, the empire and its people had peace and unity, so long desired by the philosophers of all schools. That the price of peace was a price the Chinese were never willing to offer again, at least until 1948, when the Communists took control, is another story.

Shang Yang's proposals were exciting, if for no other

reason than that they were neat, bold and plausible. They presented a peculiar problem to the mystics, in part because both schools agreed on the debacle of contemporary Chou civilization and in part because absolute autocracy itself is a mysticism of a kind.

"If, in a country," said Shang Yang, "there are the following ten things: odes and history, rites and music, virtue and the cultivation thereof, benevolence and integrity, sophistry and intelligence, then the ruler has no one whom he can employ for defense and warfare. . . . If study becomes popular, people will abandon agriculture and occupy themselves with debates, high-sounding words and discussions on false premises . . . and this leads to the impoverishment of the state." The mystics also deplored the professional talkers who went about spreading confusion with their contentions. In Poem 19, for example, agreement with the Legalists is indicated on this point but, of course, for quite different reasons.

In Poems 3 and 65, the mystics agree that telling the people too much about public policy is bad for government. Lord Shang says: "One cannot let the people share in thoughts about the beginning of an affair but they should be allowed to share in the rejoicing over the completion of it. . . . The ruler makes the people single-minded and therefore they will not scheme for selfish profit."

In Poem 61, Ch'in's population problem is discussed with apparent sympathy and understanding. The great land needs more people; the small one needs more space to work. There is a Way by which the small and great countries can serve each other's needs: let the big country be humble and quiet and immigration will flow into it like streams to the sea. But Ch'in was listening to another voice and had no intention of letting nature take its course. Perhaps it was he who (19) laughed out loud. Possibly Poems 29 and 30 were addressed to him.

There was also general agreement among the varied schools that the king must be held an absolute autocrat and, as such, considered the incarnation of the state. This is a mystical notion. Equally mystical was the belief that the character and well-being of the state and its people derived solely from the character of the monarch and his acts. Being human, as well as divine, the king usually had the limitations of his humanity; and this provided the various professors of wisdom with a rationalization of their function. At this point, the radical differences of Legalist and mystic appeared in bold outline.

"What the world now calls righteousness," says Lord Shang, "is the establishment of what people like and the abolishment of what they dislike. . . . The strong are unbending. . . . Compassion and pity in the heart cause brave people to be anxious and fearful people not to fight. . . . Punishment produces force, force produces strength, strength produces awe, awe produces virtue. Virtue has its origin in punishments." The uncompromising reply of the mystics, that virtue is derived from the unworldly Way, is the principal subject of the eighty poems of *Tao Té Ching*. A quick reference at this point to Poems 39, 43, 57 and 78 will illustrate the mystic rebuttal.

Yin-Yang

Sometime during the third century B.C., still another group developed an indigenous and probably very ancient dualism into a more or less systematic purview of nature. They became known as the "Yin-Yang" experts. Their writings have perished, but from quotations, it is known that they developed cosmological ideas and a limited amount of geographical information comparable to that of the early Ionian thinkers.

Yin and Yang are the famed cognates of Chinese thought about nature.* Generally speaking, Yin stands

*See symbol above.

for a constellation of such qualities as shade ("on the north side of a hill"), darkness, cold, negativeness, weakness, femaleness, etc.; while Yang ("on the south side of a hill") denotes light, heat, strength, positiveness, maleness, etc. The Yin-Yang experts regarded the interaction of these cognates as the explanation of all change in the universe. Not even politics was exempt: "Kuan Tzu said, The king's edicts should be seasonable; if they are unseasonable, then look out for what will come because of heaven. . . . Thus Yin and Yang are the major principles of the world, the great regulators of the four seasons. Even the moral effect of punishments has to do with the seasons; if it accords with the season, it will be beneficial; otherwise it breeds evil." (Chap. 40 of the "Kuan Tzu" Book.)

The words Yin and Yang occur only once in the *Tao Té Ching*, in Poem 42, where they are covered up to some degree by their translation as "shade" and "sun," respectively. This passage, nevertheless, bears witness to the influence of the current theory on the mystics.

Far more important is the constant occurrence throughout the book of what Dr. Roderick Scott calls "Yinism." The "valley spirit" is praised (6) and called the "mystic female." Poem 28 deals almost wholly with the mystic's preference for Yin over Yang, a remarkable point of view in a patriarchal society which exalts the male at every point, as Dr. Scott has indicated. Weakness and softness are repeatedly praised. The Wise Man is generally described as having characteristics normally associated with women. The Way itself is described (59) as a mother. Even the ideal realm is described as female (61):

> The great land is a place
> To which the streams descend;
> It is the concourse and
> The female of the world:

Quiescent, underneath,
It overcomes the male.

Which is to say, it overcomes the would-be conqueror.

A possible explanation of the Yinism of the mystics would begin with the fact that matriarchy was still remembered among the Shang. The first mystics may possibly have been recruited from the remnant of this conquered people, and the images of "the mother" (1, 52, 59) or the "mystic female" (6) may have been bright in their minds. Firsthand experimentation with the unseen world, however, would have led them to the same conclusion without the tradition of matriarchy.

Poem 67 begins with the complaint: "Everywhere, they say the Way, our doctrine, is so very like detested folly." To many people still, mysticism is folly; it makes almost no appeal to common sense and is not comprehensible short of personal experimentation. What is even worse is that it requires the surrender of dominance and purposeful action, on which men pride themselves, and asks instead for passivity before God, which is often thought to be characteristic of women. These considerations, taken together, may have influenced the literate males of ancient China to choose Confucianism, but it did not enable them to forget the mystic Way altogether.

Then too, considering the subsequent career of mysticism within Taoism, China's native organized religion, it is not surprising that it failed to win respect comparable to that achieved by Confucianism. In later centuries it became associated in the popular mind with occult matters, magic, traffic with the dead, alchemy and other mystifying feats utterly alien to its genius. Enshrined as a "ching," a sacred book of the Taoist church, the *Tao Té Ching* soon fell into honored desuetude, and the great antidote to superstition became the chief sanction of systematic superstition.

Tao Té Ching

The identity of China's mystics is complicated by the rule that no true mystic would know himself to be such. He could no more discuss mysticism at arm's length, so to speak, than the Bible could discuss religion objectively. Christ, for example, does not mention religion; he *is* religious and all he does and says is therefore religious, but not self-consciously so. We may be quite sure that the greatest of mystics knew nothing of mysticism. "If anyone wishes to walk in my footsteps, let him renounce self. . . ." (Mark 8:34.) The renunciation of self requires, among other things, that one learn to disregard his personal identity, to lose it in unself-conscious devotion to the object of his quest. This is the first rule of mysticism. The rule is somewhat differently expressed in Poem 1:

> The secret waits for the insight
> Of eyes unclouded by longing;
> Those who are bound by desire
> See only the outward container.

This, of course, is bound to lead to an unsatisfactory result for people interested in the biographical details of mystic authors. Generally speaking, in their concern for the subject of their lives, mystics neglect to mention themselves. We do not know who composed the chapters of the *Tao Té Ching*. The authorship of many another kind of writing is lost by accident; but mysticism is often given anonymously, by principle. All we can guess about the authorship of these poems is that the main threads of their argument originated among recluses in remote valleys (6) before Confucius' time and that the result took form late in the third century B.C.

Where there is no author, however, it is necessary to invent one; and by the time the *Tao Té Ching* had been put in form, legend had supplied Lao Tzu (pronounced *low* as in *allow*), and Ssu-ma Ch'ien incorporated the legend in his notable *Historical Records* (chap. 63). It presents Lao Tzu correctly enough as one who has given up civilized living and is impatient with Confucian ideas and who accordingly departs for points unknown, presumably to live out his life as a recluse.

"As for Lao Tzu," says Ssu-ma Ch'ien, "he came from the Good Will Corners section of Grindstone Village in the Hardpan district of the Moors (Ch'u). He belonged to the Plum family clan. His given name was Ear and, familiarly, he was called Uncle Sun. Posthumously, he was called Tan [pronounced *Dan* and meaning rimless ears]. He was an historian in the secret archives of Chou.

"Confucius came to Chou to consult Lao Tzu about ritual [and spoke of the heroes of old].

"Lao Tzu said, 'All those men of whom you speak have long since mouldered away with their bones. Only their words remain. When a capable man's time comes, he rises; if it does not, then he just wanders wearily around. I have heard that good merchants keep their goods buried deeply to make it look as if they had none and that a superior man whose character is perfected will feign stupidity. Give up, sir, your proud airs, your many wishes, mannerisms and extravagant claims. They won't do you any good, sir! That's all I have to tell you.'

"Confucius went off and said to his students: 'I know that birds can fly and fish can swim and beasts can run. Snares can be set for things that run, nets for those that swim and arrows for whatever flies. But dragons! I shall never know how they ride wind and cloud up into the sky. Today I saw Lao Tzu. What a dragon!'

"Lao Tzu practised the Way and its Virtue. He learned to do his work in self-effacement and anonymity. For a long time he lived in Chou, and when he saw that it was breaking up, he left. At the frontier, the official Yin Hsi said: 'Since, sir, you are retiring, I urge you to write me a book.'

"So Lao Tzu wrote a book in two parts, explaining the Way and its Virtue in something over five thousand words. Then he went away. No one knows where he died."

Ssu-ma Ch'ien's legend may very well contain the kind of truth good fiction sets forth. Mysticism in China antedated Confucius and there may have been a Lao Tan (Old Tan) who was known as Lao Tzu (The Old One or the old philosopher). Lao Tzu's lines about Confucius' manners illustrate the well-known scorn of the mystics for Confucianism. Moreover, there are signs in the *Analects* that Confucius had met and conversed with some of the mystics with negative results: "There are people with whom one can study but whom one cannot join in the Way. . . ." (*Analects* IX:29.)

It is more probable, however, that "Lao Tzu" is a pseudonym. "Lao" is not a surname but an adjective meaning "old"; and after the literary convention of the day, it would suggest that the author of the *Tao Té Ching* was not only an ancient, but was also ripe in years when he composed the masterpiece. It was a skillful choice on the part of the final authors who, after their own principles, chose anonymity and were moved to apply their cherished insight to issues that were not sharply defined until two centuries after the death of Confucius. Much of their work was not controversial. It was the careful expression of an insight that had matured slowly through the centuries.

What they had to say resulted from their own discoveries; and for our understanding, it needs comparison with the reports of mystics in other lands and other times. The remarkable unanimity of the great mystics of China, India, Persia, the Holy Lands and Europe is one of the truly impressive facts of the spiritual history of the human race. We may believe that this unanimity is due to personal causes. Generally, the great ones have begun with a deep skepticism about popular or traditional religion and man's power to influence God or the gods. Their insights have been derived from an overwhelming experience of a reality beyond themselves rather than a postulate. They have matured with moral growth rather than intellectual effort. They are usually skilled thinkers, but when they have offered explanations, the explanation is clearly a by-product, rather than an object in itself.

Wherever the great mysticism has come, it has offered to replace popular or local religion with a new and universal allegiance. Folk beliefs about gods and spirits give place to a metaphysic of the utmost generality for those who can rise to it. The mystic's passion is satisfied only with the sense of the Ultimate Reality, the God, Godhead or Godness that is back of the world of mind and nature. What is the Ultimate like? And what has it to do with man? The mystic report is that:

Reality, however designated, is One; it is an all-embracing unity from which nothing can be separated: "Hear, O Israel; the Lord our God is one Lord." (Palestine, seventh century B.C.) "So I say that likeness born of the One, leads the soul to God, for he is One, unbegotten unity, and of this we have clear evidence." (Eckhart, Germany, 1300.) "Behold but One in all things; it is the second that leads you astray." (Kabir, India, 1500.) "Something there is, whose veiled creation was before the earth or sky began to be; so silent, so aloof and so alone, it changes not, nor fails, but touches all." (*Tao Té Ching*, 25.)

IT, the Ultimate, is nameless, indescribable, beyond telling: and therefore anything said about it is faulty: ". . . What is his name? . . . And God said to Moses, I AM WHAT I AM . . . say unto the children of Israel, I AM hath sent me unto you." (Exodus 3:14.) "Describe it as form yet unformed; as shape that is still without shape; or say it is vagueness confused: one meets it and it has no front; one follows and there is no rear." (14.) "IT cannot be defined by word or idea; as the Scripture says, it is the One 'before whom words recoil.'" (Shankaracharya, India, 800.) "It is God's nature to be without a nature. To think of his goodness, or wisdom, or power is to hide the essence of him, to obscure it with thoughts about him. . . . Who is Jesus? He has no name." (Eckhart.)

Within the self, IT is to be found and there it is identical with Reality in the external world: "So God created man in his own image, in the image of God created he him. . . ." (Genesis 1:27.) ". . . the Father is in me and I in the Father. . . . I and the Father are one." (John 10:38, 30.) "As sure as the Father, so single in nature, begets his Son, he begets him in the spirit's inmost recess, and that is the inner world. Here, the core of God is also my core; and the core of my soul, the core of God's. . . ." (Eckhart.) "Here likewise in this body of yours, my son, you do not perceive the True; but there in fact it is. In that which is the subtle essence, all that exists has its self. That is the True, that is the Self, and thou, Svetaketu, are That." (Chandogya Upanishad, India.) "I went from God to God, until they cried from me in me, 'O thou I!' " (Bayazid, Persia, 847.) "The world may be known without leaving the house; The Way may be seen apart from the windows." (47.)

IT can be known, not discursively, but by acquaintance, and this acquaintance is the point of all living: "This is Life Eternal, to know you, the one true God. . . ." (John 17:3.) "Know that when you learn to lose yourself, you will reach the Beloved. There is no other secret to be learnt, and more than this is not known to me." (Ansari of Herat.) "Where is this God? In eternity. Just as a man who is in hiding clears his throat and reveals his whereabouts, so it is with God. Nobody could ever find God. He has to discover himself. . . . But when one takes God as he is divine . . . he will be like one athirst; he cannot help drinking even though he thinks of other things . . . the idea of the Drink will not depart as long as the thirst endures." (Eckhart.) "If you work by the Way, you will be of the Way; if you work through its virtue you will be given the virtue, abandon either one and both abandon you." (23.)

Reality is disclosed only to those who meet its conditions and the conditions are primarily moral: "Blessed are the pure in heart: for they shall see God." (Matthew 5:8.) "The more a man regards everything as divine—more divine than it is of itself—the more God will be pleased with him. To be sure, this requires effort and love, a careful cultivation of the spiritual life, and a watchful, honest, active oversight of all one's mental attitudes toward things and people. It is not to be learned by world-flight, running away from things, turning solitary and going apart from the world. Rather, one must learn an inner solitude. He must learn to penetrate things and find God there, to get a strong impression of God fixed firmly in his mind." (Eckhart.) "When the heart weeps for what it has lost, the spirit laughs for what it has found." (Sufi.) "With the lamp of word and discrimination one must go beyond word and discrimination and enter upon the path of realization." (Lankavantara Sutra.) "The student learns by daily increment. The Way is gained by daily loss, loss upon loss until at last comes rest." (48.)

This outline of illustrative material taken from the writings of mystics of diverse lands and times is, of course, intended only to suggest the uplands of the spirit touched by those who wrote the *Tao Té Ching*. The Chinese purview of those uplands was somewhat bleaker than that of many other great mystic writings, perhaps because the difficulties of calligraphy in ancient China demanded severe terseness. It may also have been due to certain esoteric requirements put upon its poems: they suggest that aside from the king, others for whom they were intended had already been disciplined through long renunciation to understand their cryptic references. Clearly, the Way had to be learned; it could not be taught.

On mature acquaintance, however, what at first appears as bleakness in these poems becomes a powerful simplicity of conception and a sureness of touch in which there is no waste motion. What can be said of the Way is said with great economy of language, an economy like that of lightning in the night. The Virtue or power of the Way is illustrated by an assertion of the consequences of letting the Way be the way by which the affairs of men are dispatched. This is the radical element in the poems. Reality, the Way, is taken with great seriousness. Why should men interfere with its operations? It would be much better if, from the king down to the least peasant, the wills of men should be held subject to the Way, so that like all else in the universe, men should become its perfect instruments. Let be! Then the mighty Way will act through you and its power will accomplish what you cannot do of your own volition.

Does all the plotting and planning, the fetching and carrying, the making and unmaking which comprise the life of the world make for good? Is there progress toward a better world which is the fruit of human hearts and hands? When the Chou supplanted the Shang, their answer to such questions was decidedly in the affirmative. And plainly, even God agreed. Had he not withdrawn his mandate from Shang and given it to Chou? Six centuries later there was doubt about it. Men saw themselves the victims of natural calamities, even politics and war, against which they were powerless to contrive a remedy. Was there a remedy? Confucius answered in the affirmative. There was a remedy in the efforts of the moral man. Others, without saying either yes or no, went off to the mountain valleys to consider their answer. They became recluses, the first mystics.

Chinese Mystics

Men do not flee civilized society and commit themselves to the rough embrace of mother nature unless their distress is deep or their delusions are overpowering. In either case, they run the risk of being reduced to anthropoids, if they survive at all. Perhaps it was one of these who appeared to Confucius one day with a method in his madness:

"The mad carriage-greeter of Ch'u came past Confucius' carriage, singing as he walked:

> The phoenix, the phoenix!
> His prestige has gone down!
> Don't say he hasn't tried:
> For he may get there yet:
> But he should quit,
> Oh, he should quit:
> It's much too dangerous
> In politics today!

Confucius got out of the carriage to speak to him but he ran and got away, so that Confucius had no chance to talk to him." (*Analects* XVIII:5.)

The so-called madman's raillery, in his reference to Confucius as the "phoenix," a mythical bird of good omen, is often taken as evidence that the story was anti-Confucian propaganda. Its inclusion in the *Analects,* however, is sufficient proof that it is not necessarily so. More probably, it records just one of the incidents of Confucius' travels, as he went about seeking employment by some prince. The "madman" is thought to have been one of the early recluses who gained license by feigning madness. His song was strictly in the tenor of mysticism and illustrates the humble beginnings of the movement.

The first Chinese mystic to receive personal notice was Yang Chu, about whom we know little. He seems to have been born about forty years after Confucius' death and to have drawn fire from the eminent Confucian Mencius (372?–289?):

"The words of Yang Chu and Mo Ti fill the world! . . . Mr. Yang's doctrine of *wei wo* [literally, *for me*] is anarchical . . . and beast-like. . . . If the doctrines of Yang and Mo are not stopped and those of Confucius are not published, their mad talk will deceive the people and put an end to goodness and justice and we shall go back to the jungles and cannibalism. . . . When Wise Men once more arise, they will not change what I have said. . . ." (*Mencius,* III B 9.)

Such strong talk from so prominent a teacher may account for the paucity of material which has survived from Yang Chu even at secondhand. Clearly, Mencius and others misunderstood his phrases and this alone should keep a modern interpreter humble. But Yang Chu had something new to say and old words to say it with. Dimly it appears that as Confucius had discovered the moral man, Yang Chu discovered that individual people could have a life of their own, one by one, apart from the society into which they were born. The discovery of the individual may have been the fruit of the lonely vigils of the valley recluses, but it fell to Yang Chu to put the new idea of individualism into words. He chose *wei wo,* which in modern Chinese means *selfishness,* and accordingly led many critics astray. It led even the great Mencius astray: "Yang Tzu fixed on *wei wo*: he would not have given a single hair of his head to benefit the world." (*Mencius,* VII A 25.)

It is from Huai-nan Tzu, a mystic writer of the second century, that more favorable and, we may hope, truer notice of Yang Chu's doctrines is had. Evidently Yang Chu had observed the world of nature at length and admired its effortless course. He seems to have felt that it would be good for man to be like nature in this respect.

Two other phrases from Yang Chu are indicative, even though his precise meaning is beyond reach: *Yang Sheng* and *Ch'üan Sheng. Yang* is the principle of the sun, and *Sheng* is life, so that a fair guess at the meaning of the phrase might be "glorify life." *Ch'üan* means "to perfect, to complete," and the second phrase thus might mean "perfect your life" so that it proceeds effortlessly, as nature does. If these conjectures are correct, Yang Chu did indeed make notable contributions to the view that finally inspired the *Tao Té Ching*.

The second great contributor to mystic theory was Chuang Chou (369?–286?). Once again, we know very little of him personally, except what we can read between the lines of what he wrote. His vivid imagination, his strong logical mind, his wit and humor, and, more generally, his powers as a poet are apparent to all who read his literary remains. From the point of view of his influence on subsequent Chinese thought and art, his most important contribution was made through a poetic glorification of nature that has excited Chinese landscapists ever since. The recluses, for example, are transmuted into "mountain men" (fairies) to illustrate what the virtue of the Way can do through one who is pure in heart: "Inquiring of Lien Shu, Chien Wu said, 'I heard Chieh Yü say . . . that a spirit man lives over on the Miao-ku-she mountain. His skin and flesh are like ice and snow; he is gentle and demure like a girl; he eats no ordinary food; he sucks the wind and sips the dew. He mounts clouds in the air and drives a team of flying dragons out beyond the four seas. A congealed ghost, he nevertheless delivers living things from corruption and makes the crops ripen year by year. I consider this crazy and do not believe it.' 'Indeed,' said Lien Shu, 'blind men have no conception of art, nor can the deaf conceive the sound of bells or drums.' " (*Chuang Tzu,* chap. 1.)

At the tip of his brush, freedom is depicted in terms of a fabulous whale which turns into a bird of corresponding size, requiring a thousand miles of ocean for its take-off and then flies six months before coming to rest.

The thirty-one chapters of the *Chuang Tzu* text are really an anthology of such literary feats, intermingled with prose discourse. The collection reveals how diversely the Chinese mystics were influenced by other schools of thought and how the mystics of a given locality of the world can vary among themselves. The contributions of the *Chuang Tzu* text are also by no means of one date. Some of them are quite old, while others must be much later in origin than Chuang Tzu's own writings.

His version of the Way led him into fatalism, a fatalism which the writers of the *Tao Té Ching* outgrew, but which Chuang Tzu could clothe with romantic beauty. Speaking of the death of Lao Tzu: "When he happened to come, it was the Master's time to come; when he happened to go, he went, of course. Given calm acceptance of the time and place for everything, neither grief nor joy can intrude. . . . The fingers tire feeding twigs to the fire but the fire is passed on and when it will die out no one knows." (*Ibid.*, chap. 3.)

The basic mystic assertion that Reality is One also led Chuang Tzu to some hard conclusions, under the general topic: The Harmony of Things. The harmony of things meant the leveling out of distinctions of every kind, even those on which civilization and morality are based. Chuang Tzu, like many another mystic, took a dim view of civilization as an artificial state in which life was labor and sorrow to no discernible end: "To wear out one's soul trying to understand the oneness of things and not to know their identity, this I call 'Three in the Morning.' What do I mean by that? Well, when a monkey-keeper was passing out the chestnuts, he said, 'Three in the morning and four in the evening.' That made all the monkeys angry. So he said, 'All right, then, four in the morning and three in the evening.' The monkeys were all pleased." (*Ibid.*, chap. 2.)

Among mystics of every land and time, there have been persons prone to ecstatic experiences, sometimes involuntary and sometimes deliberately induced. Off in the valleys, where the recluses forgot the busy world, long before anything was known of Indian Yoga, the Chinese mystics evidently experimented with trances. Simply by sitting still and concentrating on *anything,* they learned the art of *Tso-wang,* "sitting abstraction," about which any practiced sitting-thinker knows very well without being a mystic at all. In even so mild a trance as this, they were quiet, effortless, alone, and knew an indescribable pleasure, sometimes of pure fantasy, sometimes of insight that amounted to revelation. This must have been the origin of the principle of *Wu-wei,* deliberate inactivity, quietism, by which the self was voided and the Way took over one's being and doing.

Others, however, experimented with deeper retreats from the world of sense, in a search for "that whereby one knows." Several passages in the *Chuang Tzu* text illustrate how this was accomplished, apparently by a system of breath-control, although probably some adepts were naturally given to such practices: "Tzu Ch'i, a man from South Suburbs, sat down, leaning against a bench and looking up at the sky. Slowly he let out his breath. Oblivious to everything, he seemed to lose part of himself. Yen Ch'eng Tzu Yu [his disciple] who was standing there to wait on him said, 'What's this? You make your body like dry wood and your mind like dead ashes! The man now leaning against the bench is not the one who leaned against it a while ago.' Tzu Ch'i said, 'Isn't a lull a good thing? As for your question, you know the answer: just now, I lost me.' " (*Ibid.,* chap. 2.)

The *Tao Té Ching* shows (10) at least a vestigial interest in breath-control as a means to quietness, through which virtue or power is released. To be still and to know the Way for what it is, was the avowed object of those poems, but Yoga practices are not surely intended. And here the reader's own judgment is required. If the *Tao Té Ching* is classed as first rate among mystic writings, it is a fair assumption that while ecstatic trances and their pleasures are accepted as legitimate symptoms of union with Reality, they are by no means the best evidence that such a union has been achieved. "If such things (trances) are really due to God, he gives them to people to bait them and allure them on and also to keep them away from worse company. But when such people increase in love, ecstatic experiences will come less facilely, and the love that is in them will be proved by the constancy of their fidelity to God, without such enticements." (Meister Eckhart.)

This is the general tenor of the poems of the *Tao Té Ching,* and explains the single reference (10) to physically contrived stillness. The great stillness that invites invasion by the Way, and from which Virtue emerges, is other than physical.

There are a number of parallel sayings and passages in *Chuang Chou* and the *Tao Té Ching.* On the assumption that Chuang Chou's work is the earlier, the parallel passages in the later work might be taken as quotations, generally polished and expanded. Both works agree that the Way is ineffable (1), that it is a void beyond filling (4), that color debauches the eye (12), that government can be entrusted to the disinterested lover of the world (13), that wisdom and learning should be done away with (19), that wise men should be kept out of sight (36), that the one begot two, and two, three . . . (42), that the highest skill is like clumsiness (45), and that the ideal land is most primitive (80).

The earlier work often erupts; for Chuang Chou was geyser-like. By the time the *Tao Té Ching* was assembled, the impulse to erupt was curbed somewhat by the desire to give the wisdom accumulated over several centuries more careful statement and, accordingly, the matter and form of portions of the poems offer an analogy to the eternal marriage of the Way and its virtue, which they describe.

Key Concepts

Before a final description of the content of the work is undertaken, a consideration of the meaning of some of its key words is necessary.

道 TAO. A road, a path, the way by which people travel, the way of nature and finally the Way of ultimate Reality. The Chinese character is composed of a head, representing a knowing person, and another part that primitively depicted the process of walking. It is impossible to say how old some of the overtones of the word are. Certainly it had a limited meaning for Confucius; but to the Chinese mystics, it came not only to refer to the way the whole world of nature operates but to signify the original undifferentiated Reality from which the universe is evolved.

In Chinese, nouns often become verbs at the pleasure of the user. Thus, in Poem 1, line 1, Tao, the Way, is used both as a noun and a verb. Literally, therefore, one could translate these two famed first lines as follows:

The way that can be way-ed is not the eternal Way; The name that can be named is not the real Name. This is picturesque and would be familiar to many lovers of these poems and will serve as a background for comparison with the rendering I have given.

It may be helpful in understanding the meaning that crept by degrees into this originally simple Chinese word to compare it to the ultimate Reality Plato described as The Good:

"You will agree that the Sun not only makes the things we see visible, but also brings them into existence and gives them growth and nourishment; yet he is not the same thing as existence. And so with the objects of knowledge: these derive from the Good not only their power of being known, but their very being and reality; and Goodness is not the same thing as being, but even beyond being, surpassing it in dignity and power." (*Republic* VI:508.)

The Way corresponds to the medieval conception of Godhead or Godness, which also might be called "a preface to God" (4):

"God enjoys himself in everything. . . . Thus creatures speak of God—but why do they not mention the Godhead? Because there is only unity in the Godhead and there is nothing to talk about. God acts. The Godhead does not. It has nothing to do and there is nothing going on in it. It is never on the lookout for something to do. The difference between God and the Godhead is the difference between action and non-action." (Meister Eckhart.)

Another and more familiar parallel is to be found in the *logos* or Word of the gospel of John: "In the beginning was the Word, and the Word was with God, and the Word was God." (1:1) Even better, the Word, the Way, later in the fourth gospel, is made intelligible and practicable: "Jesus saith unto him, I am the way. . . ."

德 TÊ. Virtue, character, influence, moral force. The character consists of three parts, (1) an ideograph meaning "to go"; (2) another, meaning "straight"; and (3) a picturograph meaning "the heart." Put together, these signify motivation by inward rectitude. The *Shuo Wen Chieh Tzu* (Explanation of words and analysis of characters), a dictionary of the second century A.D., quoting earlier works, defines *Té* as "the outward effect of a man and the inward effect of the self."

Undoubtedly, in primitive times in China, as elsewhere, there was a magical *virtus,* virtue or power which belonged to certain things, each in its own way, and especially to people, some of whom had it to such a degree that they could work miracles. As such, virtue had no necessary overtone of morality. By the time of Confucius, however, *Té,* though still a force around people and things, somewhat suggestive of the magnetic or gravitational field, had become unmistakably moral in nature:

"Someone asked, 'What do you think of requiting enmity with virtue?' The Master replied, 'How then would you reward virtue? Reward enmity with justice and virtue with virtue.' " (*Analects* XIV:36.)

The idea of virtue as a force, moral or otherwise, has not departed from modern languages as, for example, in the expression, "By virtue of its strength, steel is useful." One would therefore expect the idea of force to be present in the usage of the *Tao Té Ching.*

The predominant overtone of the word is, nevertheless, moral: If the king will proceed according to the Way, his virtue will appear (67), as courage, frugality and humility.

The parallel thought in the gospels is illustrative. When sick people pressed around him, Jesus felt power or virtue go out of him (Luke 6:19; 8:46.); but in the long run, it was the Holy Spirit, sent in his name, the spirit of truth, that would inform his disciples. (John 15.)

為無為 *Wei wu wei.* This paradoxical expression is the key to Chinese mysticism. It cannot be translated literally and still render its meaning. *Wei* is a verb corresponding to the English *do* or *act* but sometimes meaning other things, depending on the expression. *Wu* is a negative. Thus, clumsily, *wei wu wei* is *to do without doing, to act without action.* Put positively, it means to get along as nature does: the world gets created, living things grow and pass away without any sign of effort.

More exactly, *Wu wei* is man's part; he is to be still, quiet and passive so that the *Way,* ultimate Reality, the universe of being, may act through him without let or hindrance. The first *wei* is then the part of the Way. To use more familiar vocabulary, the idea is *to let God be God in you.* The result, we are assured, is incalculable accomplishment, but it might not be any civilization man has achieved to date.

Wei wu wei occurs many times in the *Tao Té Ching.* It has to be translated in almost as many different ways. There are three other related expressions worth comment: *Tzu-jan, P'o* and *Pu shih.*

自然 *Tzu-jan.* Naturally, of itself; from *tzu,* self, and *jan,* an adverbial suffix (ly); what happens of itself, without prompting and therefore spontaneously. This expression may be taken as the positive version of *wu wei.* In the discussions of the *Tao Té Ching,* the analogy is always from nature, as if these poets too were saying: "Consider the lilies of the field, how they grow." Nature is spontaneous; men should be spontaneous also and it is the Way's virtue that makes them so, when they yield to it.

樸 *P'o.* A kind of tree and hence a "virgin block" of wood, untooled, and not artificial; raw material and thence, the natural state of things: substance, plain, simple, sincere. This word is probably an old technical term of the mystics who dwelt long with "untouched nature" before their views were committed to written words. Its use is to urge men to put away the artificial manners of civilization so that honesty and sincerity may be possible once again. *P'o* is also a symbol of the *Way and its Virtue.* It is sometimes a synonym for *wu wei* and a model of *tzu-jan.*

不恃 *Pu shih.* To be independent, not involved with things or affairs, aloof. This expression carries out the meaning of *wu wei.* The Wise Man does what he has to do for everything and everybody but remains independent of them all. He is, therefore, the absolute autocrat.

無名 *Wu ming.* Without a name, nameless, and so without any distinguishing features to which a name can be given. The phrase is frequently used to describe the Way and its effects. It therefore designates "unique," since a name can be given to anything that is not unique. Thus, because the Way is unique, no known names apply to it and it cannot be described.

愛 *Ai.* This word usually means "love" but has retained a more primitive meaning: to want for one's self and hence, to begrudge, to be stingy, to covet. In this sense, it occurs in Poem 44, where it is translated as "mean."

聖人 *Sheng Jen.* The Wise Man, the sage. Etymologically *Sheng* means the duty to listen (to the voice of wisdom) and to say then what one has heard. It hardly corresponds to "holy" and *Sheng Jen* is not to be translated as "the holy man," but there is an element of reverence in the expression.

One nice anecdote illustrates how thoroughly the expression has been considered. A wayfarer met a Wise Man one day and said to him,

"Sir, are you a Wise Man?"

Whereupon the Wise Man bowed in thought awhile and then replied,

"If I say that I *am* a Wise Man, then obviously I am *not;* but if I say that I am not a Wise Man, I shall not be telling the truth!"

The Wise Man is mentioned, as such, sixty times in the text of the poems in such a way that it is a fair conjecture that the expression is a euphuism for "king." In Poems 3, 49, and 66 the use of "the Wise Man" clearly shows that a king is indicated. Other poems point to the same conclusion, as does 26, where the inference is that the Wise Man rules ten thousand chariots. Accordingly, the assumption is justified that these poems amount to open letters to a king. Aside from this, today the reader can be king; the poems are politely recommended to him.

天 *T'ien.* God, heaven, the sky. The most ancient forms of *t'ien* are picturographic, showing a human figure complete with a head, two arms and two legs. It may have represented the supreme ancestor, in its earliest uses. By some process of extension it came also to designate the sky, the abode of the ancestors and so, "heaven," the community of the departed.

Confucius uses the term in much the same sense as "God"; Mo Ti, Chuang Tzu and others do the same. If one asks whether *T'ien* means God, it is necessary to ask then what "God" means. Obviously the word "God" means many things to many people. Sometimes the conception of God is anthropomorphic; sometimes it is personal in a subtler sense; sometimes it is a purely impersonal term. Undoubtedly, the same variations in meaning apply to *T'ien*.

In the *Tao Té Ching, T'ien* is personal except when it obviously means "sky." In Chinese mysticism, then, the Way, like the Godhead of medieval Europe, is like a preface to God (4).

The *Tao Té Ching* as a whole is a collection or perhaps an anthology. It consists of instructional pieces, hymns, polemic fragments and proverbs. It achieves some degree of unity because it is edited from the point of view of an established but informal cult. It is probable that some passages are quite old, but these are not surely discernible. The editors seem to have proceeded on the principle of *tzu-jan,* spontaneity, and the whole work is as artless as the Virginal Block. Its power is due to the economy and obvious sincerity with which its great insights are expressed; it never wavers and it contains very little extraneous matter.

We have also seen that much of what is reported in the *Tao Té Ching* is parallel to the discoveries of mystics elsewhere in the world. The Way might well be Brahman's brother. There is, however, no reason to believe that its ideas were imported from India, although suggestions to that effect have been made from time to time. Its thought is native, unmistakably so, but not local. What these mystics found turned out to be as true in one country as another and as trustworthy a guide to the spiritual world today as then. Some of them must have been highly gifted men, and all were moved to discover a resource able to deliver mankind from evil. Clearly, they were satisfied that deliverance was not to be found on the level of magic or ritual, or through the childish devices of greedy, fearful men. It should not be astonishing that their insights were like those of mystics in other lands. Their natures were not unique; nor did the problem of evil as they met it differ essentially from that of other lands.

Their solution came with protracted observation of

the world of nature and their conclusion was that the Way of nature is the ultimate Reality that gives birth to all things and regulates them. The Way of nature is the universe of being, with this difference: it is process and not static. So much might be gathered from the word chosen to designate it. The Way is not a path which nature might take, but is the movement of nature itself; it is an effortless movement, but nonetheless a movement, like the annual rhythm of the seasons:

> I do not know its name;
> A name for it is "Way";
> Pressed for designation,
> I call it Great.
> Great means outgoing,
> Outgoing, far-reaching,
> Far-reaching, return. (25, also 16.)

It is not only nature's Way; it is also God's Way, the way God himself operates (77, 81). In light of the remark (4) that the Way is like "a preface to God," we might wonder whether the Way is prior to God or an approach to him. This question must go unanswered. Mysticism is not theology and the Chinese mystics made no pretense of being theologians. There was the Way; there was God; it was God's Way; it was nature's Way. God, the Way and nature together were One (39).

The Way, accordingly, could not be conceived as a vast, neutral blob of Being. God being involved, men also were involved, at first potentially and then by obligation. Like all else in the world, man is produced by the Way, and before he is born, he exists in the Way like a form without form (21):

> The Way itself is like some thing
> Seen in a dream. . . .
> In it are images, elusive, evading one.

> In it are things like shadows in twilight.
> In it are essences, subtle but real,
> Embedded in truth.

The ultimate Reality is therefore not impersonal; to coin a word, it is proto-personal, that is, pregnant like a mother (1) with men as well as things. It is One and God is in it; it therefore involves personality.

The Way not only gives to each thing its being or existence; it also gives to each its appropriate virtue. In the case of inanimate objects this virtue is probably best understood as meaning properties (39). In the case of man, virtue means character, the moral character which defines a man as a person. In order to obtain the Virtue of the Way, man must surrender to it: it will not come to him automatically. Though masculine, he must learn the passivity of a female (28) and, denying himself, let the Way be his way. He must learn his own "quiet being" (*Wu wei*) before he can have the Virtue that comes of the quiet Being of the Way.

But when a man does learn to live and work by the Way, by its Virtue, he becomes a wise man, one of the "realm's edged tools," effective because his moral character is complete. Among these is *the* Wise Man, the chief, the king; and the king is the final evidence of the Way's Virtue in the world. He is the exemplar of the realm. His virtue is the paramount concern of the *Tao Té Ching*. In the universe four things are great: the Way, the sky, the earth and the king (25), but the king alone can be admonished.

The king is also alone among the four greats in needing admonition: he alone can depart from the Way. When he does depart from it, his departure results in death for him and disaster for his people. The king is immune to evil only so long as Virtue qualifies him as the Wise Man (55). What happens when the king, and therefore his people, abandon the Way is poignantly set forth in Poems 18 and 38, where the decline of the Way occasions the appearance of morality with hypocrisy and chaos in its train. It may be that these two poems were polemics against the extensive moralizing of the Confucianists. More probable is the view that they were directed against what had already been seen as ineluctable evils of civilization.

One must make due allowance for the dramatic language of mystics: it was their way to "conceive vividly." In their criticism of civilized society and its evils, for example, their words sound like an outright call to the renunciation of the life and work of centuries and a return to an unimaginable primitive mode of existence. Actually, what they contemplated was short of that and amounted to rural village life as described in Poem 80. Certainly the proscription of civilization altogether was not intended, for men are not generally solitary, or even potentially so, as the mystics well knew. The fecundity of the Way was quite equal to providing for the social order (54).

Evidently they had small faith in the knowledge conveyed by language. The written word was still relatively new in the world, and the aura about the characters impelled the few who had time for such things to memorize the words rather than to understand them, which was often quite troublesome. The mystics, moreover, were used to knowledge by acquaintance and preferred that. Through long living alone with nature, they knew nature and they knew its Way. This all-important kind of knowledge was not transmitted by the written word, even at its best. They were therefore prepared (80) to do away with writing and induce people to return to the use of knotted cords. Or were they? The fact that the *Tao Té Ching* got written down at all would seem to belie the primitivism of some of the more dramatic proposals.

Not only the Chou preferred civilized life to the ways of wild tribes against whom they were continually defending themselves: the wild tribes themselves were attracted by the civilized communities as if by tropism. In their time, the Chou had despoiled the Shang because the Shang civilization seemed so desirable. Once civilized, however, people found a new estate in which gentler garments and manners only thinly disguised still savage hearts. Then they remembered that if life was cruel in the former estate, at least it was not polluted with the host of new sins and guilts that came with civilization.

Can men be civilized, humane, and still be delivered from the evils for which sin and guilt provide the occasions? The answer of the mystics was an interesting parallel to that of St. Paul: "If it had not been for the law, I should not have known sin." (Romans 7:7.) "But if you are led of the Spirit, you are not under the law." (Galatians 5:18.) The Jewish law defined an ever increasing number of human actions as sinful; the ever expanding moral code of the Confucianists and the laws of the Legalists accomplished much the same result. In either case, civilization became an inward burden hard to bear; and, increasingly, men were guilty of lawless acts prompted by the desire for a freedom they remembered dimly as their original right. This way chaos came and freedom departed. The remedy, said St. Paul, was submission to Christ, from which all necessary social and individual virtues followed naturally, and the result would be a new liberty more secure than men had ever known. The *Tao Té Ching* contains essentially the same kind of proposal: find your deliverance by submitting to the Way: its Virtue will set you free.

The disadvantage from which the mystics of Chou (or Ch'in) suffered was that their exemplar had to be the reigning king, for whom the mystics' advice was generally lost in the babel of admonitory "wise men." Moreover, as Socrates observed:

". . . no man . . . honestly striving against the many lawless and unrighteous deeds which are done in a state, will save his life; he who would fight for the right, if he would live even for a brief space, must have a private station and not a public one." (*Apology* 32.)

The king could not be Christ; and Christ could not be the head of a state.

In the holocaust of revolution by which China was born under the "First Emperor" in 221 B.C., the *Tao Té Ching* won some favor because the dictator found in it bits of doctrine which seemed to support his program. His laws would be framed "according to the Way." He too felt that it was better to hold the people to simplicity and ignorance (3, 65). His reasons would, of course, have been quite different from those of the mystics. For the autocrat, the simple ignorance of the people would make them easier to control; for the mystics, it would allow the Way room to demonstrate its political virtue. Moreover, since the dawn of civilization, few if any have been bold enough to assume autocratic rule without some sanction beyond that of naked force. The modern dictator rules in the name of the "people"; kings used to rule by "divine right"; undoubtedly the first emperor of China wanted to feel that he ruled by the Way: then the people would believe in him and he in himself. So he favored the mystics because, though all schools made reference to the Way, none did so as impressively as they.

These considerations raise the question as to whether or no there is a natural connection between mysticism and autocracy. The *Tao Té Ching* indicates a negative answer, except as the king is enough of a Wise Man to follow its precepts. It uses the analogies of female passivity, and the lowly adaptability of water, in setting forth the basic traits of those who travel by the Way: humility, nonaction, nonassertion, forgiveness, and benevolence to all. Autocrats, as such, would naturally find these virtues difficult, if not impossible. Nor would they find the pacifist sentiments of such Poems as 30 and 31 practicable. In Poem 73, the king is advised to stop short of fancying himself God's particular instrument. In Poem 74, capital punishment, a time-honored defensive weapon of autocrats, is shown to be a liability to the king. It should be quite clear that the Ch'in autocrat's espousal of this mysticism must have been unilateral.

Considering that the objective of great mysticism

is union with God, it is hardly strange that mystics themselves should exhibit small interest in personal immortality. Poem 32 reaches its climax in an inspired quatrain that illustrates the irrelevance of immortality as the world generally conceives it:

> In this world,
> Compare those of the Way
> To torrents that flow
> Into river and sea.

Perhaps this is another special meaning to be included in the idea of "return" (16, 25). Man came from the One; he returns to the One. Otherwise, in the *Tao Té Ching* there are two brief and enigmatic references to immortality, one of which is quite consistent with the immortality involved in union with God, and the other (59) which may or may not indicate a lingering wisp of interest in individual survival. From the standpoint of popularity, this also was a disadvantage.

Near the end of the second century A.D., when mystics organized themselves into a church, the *Tao Té Ching* was promoted to the status of sacred scripture, to be read by those who had the inclination and the capacity to do so. It was too difficult for popular use and lacked, as we have seen, what people generally want: an exemplar and a picturable promise for the future of the individual. The new religion borrowed the great name and became Tao Chiao, the religion of the Way, or simply Taoism (pronounced, Dow-ism).

"Taoism," writes Dr. L. C. Goodrich, "organized into a corporate whole the original primitive beliefs and customs, those that centered about the worship of nature, which was considered animate. . . . The Tao, or Way, was the road one travelled in order to obtain three ultimate aims: happiness, wealth and long life. The intellectuals could do this by meditating on the writings of the masters and following their intellectual teachings and by consciously seeking longevity through studying alchemy and observing certain physical requirements, such as selective diet, breathing exercises, calisthenics and sexual practices. The common people could believe in the existence of ghosts and in the magic of charms; they recited parts of the slowly accumulating scriptures, and were taught to confess their sins and receive absolution by doing such good deeds as repairing a road for a length of a hundred paces. They could follow the practices prescribed for intellectuals if they could master them. Faith in the powers of magic to cure illness was held out. . . ."*

Perhaps the most notable contribution of the Taoists in subsequent centuries was a by-product of alchemy, which became an important department of their total activities. As in Europe, the object was the transmutation of base metals into gold and the production of immortality pills. As in Europe, their success with these projects was not notable, but they made incidental and important discoveries in medicine and industry; they explored human anatomy, developed chemical compounds, metallurgy, gunpowder, anaesthetics and pharmaceuticals.

From the third century A.D. on, the subsequent story of Taoism is mainly concerned with the rivalry of Buddhism. The two religions were much alike, except that Buddhism barred sexual practices, and its priests, for the most part, were celibate. Buddhism was, possibly, more popular among the "hundred clans," that is, the people; Taoism succeeded somewhat better among the literate ruling classes. It suffered at least a partial eclipse under the Mongols who favored Buddhism, and then had a revival under the Mings, perhaps because Buddhism and the Mongols were foreign, while Taoism and the Mings were indigenous.

The *Tao Té Ching* through the centuries has never been without admiring readers among the Chinese, although its reading public has been small compared to that of the Confucian books. In a land where few

*From *A Short History of the Chinese People* by L. C. Goodrich, pp. 65–66. Copyright, 1943, by Harper & Brothers.

learned to read with comprehension, Confucian writing was abstruse enough; the great mystic writing tended to be matter for scholars. Much of its message, however, found its way into the thoughts of humble people, and the contribution of the ancient mystics to the mind of China has been significant, even though a poor second to that of Confucianism.

In the matter of general interpretation, there have been many able students who have viewed the *Tao Té Ching* as naturalism, or at most as nature mysticism, staying on the materialistic side. My own view, that it is part of the great mysticism which has appeared in many parts of the world, may represent a minority report. It is based in part on what I read in the poems and in part on my own observation of the Chinese people. They are said to be notably a "practical" people, whose usages in religion have purely "practical" aims. But I have never been sure just what the word "practical" means when used in this context.

It has been my observation that, quite apart from practical considerations, the Chinese do not differ greatly from any other people in religious capacity. I see no reason why the great mysticism, which has been the life-giving urge in other lands, should not also have appeared in China. At any rate, the *Tao Té Ching* is evidence that mysticism was important in China once, and the continued interest in its scripture indicates that it can be so again. The message of the book is still of general interest, and that is important in a day when the old compartmentalization of the world is so shaken by the idea of "One World." In "One World" the *Tao Té Ching* would be quite at home.

TAO TÉ CHING

1

There are ways but the Way is uncharted;
There are names but not nature in words:
Nameless indeed is the source of creation
But things have a mother and she has a name.

The secret waits for the insight
Of eyes unclouded by longing;
Those who are bound by desire
See only the outward container.

These two come paired but distinct
By their names.
Of all things profound,
Say that their pairing is deepest,
The gate to the root of the world.

PARAPHRASE

None of the ways observed or described by us, in
which things happen or events occur, is the Master
Way by which nature works. No word or name can
disclose nature's deepest secret. Creation began in an
event which is not identified and therefore has no
name. All creatures, nevertheless, can be traced to a
common mother or matrix, something to which such
words as "mother" or "matrix" can be applied.

Nature's secret, the constant, normative Way from
which no event is exempt, is disclosed only to those
who can be rid of personal wishes or prejudices about
it. One comes to grips with it, as it lies hidden beneath
appearances, by disregarding his own point of view.
Prejudiced eyes are stopped cold at the surface.

The secret and its containers are separated only by
imagination and abstraction. In nature they are invari-
ably paired. This pairing of meaning, or principle, or life
with matter is the most profound feature of the world.
It is the clue to the understanding of all existence.

2

Since the world points up beauty as such,
There is ugliness too.
If goodness is taken as goodness,
Wickedness enters as well.

For is and is-not come together;
Hard and easy are complementary;
Long and short are relative;
High and low are comparative;
Pitch and sound make harmony;
Before and after are a sequence.

Indeed the Wise Man's office
Is to work by being still;
He teaches not by speech
But by accomplishment;
He does for everything,
Neglecting none;
Their life he gives to all,
Possessing none;
And what he brings to pass
Depends on no one else.
As he succeeds,
He takes no credit
And just because he does not take it,
Credit never leaves him.

PARAPHRASE

The palace rises in beauty only against the ugliness
of the dwellings of the poor; man's goodness is at-
tended by his wickedness.

So, generally, positive and negative, being and nonbeing, pleasant and unpleasant, good and bad, such
qualities and values come in pairs. They are relative
to human feelings; they arise from individual points of
view. They do not appear in the Way and its Virtue.

So the king does nothing of himself; he is quiet, and lets the Way act through him. He takes no pay in any form, neither fame, nor service, nor property, nor personal power, and since he does not, they all come to him.

3

If those who are excellent find no preferment,
The people will cease to contend for promotion.
If goods that are hard to obtain are not favored,
The people will cease to turn robbers or bandits.
If things much desired are kept under cover,
Disturbance will cease in the minds of the people.

The Wise Man's policy, accordingly,
Will be to empty people's hearts and minds,
To fill their bellies, weaken their ambition,
Give them sturdy frames and always so,
To keep them uninformed, without desire,
And knowing ones not venturing to act.

Be still while you work
And keep full control
Over all.

COMMENT

Mo Ti (chap. 8) blamed the poverty and disorder of the country on the failure of kings and dukes to promote the best people to office. Shang Yang opposèd the promotion of such people because it would distract them from agriculture and war, which are the nation's essential industries. Confucius had suggested that those who are free from the love of wealth would never be robbed. (*Analects* XII:18.)

The mystic's advice to the king sounds as if he sided with the legalist Shang Yang. Later poems will make it abundantly clear that he does not. His present motive is his own: to get people to abandon the vices of civilization.

The king's policy, accordingly, should aim at stilling individual appetites and ambitions among the people, even as he stills his own, so that the virtue of the Way may show in all. The king must set the example and lead the way. He will be in complete control as the Way controls him.

4

The Way is a void,
Used but never filled:
An abyss it is,
Like an ancestor
From which all things come.

It blunts sharpness,
Resolves tangles;
It tempers light,
Subdues turmoil.

A deep pool it is,
Never to run dry!
Whose offspring it may be
I do not know:
It is like a preface to God.

PARAPHRASE

Like "empty" space, the Way contains everything
and yet is never filled. Things come out of it as from
a bottomless hole, as if they were begotten there.
(Chuang Tzu's lines are parallel: "Pour into the Way:
it will not be filled. Pour out of it: you can never
exhaust it. No one knows where its contents come
from and so it is spoken of as the 'containing light.' ")
    The Way has the quality of softening all harshness.
    Looking down into its unfathomable depths, I do
not know who brought it to be but perhaps it is
God's arena.

5

Is then the world unkind?
And does it treat all things
Like straw dogs used in magic rites?
The Wise Man too, is he unkind?
And does he treat the folk
Like straw dogs made to throw away?

Between the earth and sky
The space is like a bellows,
Empty but unspent.
When moved its gift is copious.

Much talk means much exhaustion;
Better far it is to keep your thoughts!

COMMENT

The first stanza consists of statements reflecting
long-standing revolt against heaven. Life had become
bitter, as the *Book of Odes* revealed. (See Introduction.) Here, the familiar outcry includes the earth in
addition to heaven. I have translated these lines as
questions and imagined that they were uttered as sympathetic inquiry, to which the second stanza is an
answer.

Other interpreters have read this poem as indicating
that both the world and the Wise Man are quite impersonal, caring nothing for the individual and dealing
only with general situations. This seems to me foreign
to the total outlook of the *Tao Té Ching*.

The "straw dogs" offered an easily recognizable
metaphor for something worthless. Straw dogs were
used in sacrificial rites and then discarded. The ety-
mology of 獻 *hsien,* Chinese for an oblation, indicates
that dogs were once used as sacrifices in religious ritual. The straw dog was an economy.

6

The valley spirit is not dead:
They say it is the mystic female.
Her gateway is, they further say,
The base of earth and heaven.

Constantly, and so forever,
Use her without labor.

PARAPHRASE

There is a spirit that haunts the valleys that mystics know. It has the female characteristic of preferring to withdraw. It is like a gateway through which man attains heaven; and heaven reaches man when he is receptive to its nature and open to its influence.

To be open and receptive to the Way is to be useful without working at it.

7

The sky is everlasting
And the earth is very old.
Why so? Because the world
Exists not for itself;
It can and will live on.

The Wise Man chooses to be last
And so becomes the first of all;
Denying self, he too is saved.
For does he not fulfillment find
In being an unselfish man?

PARAPHRASE

The impersonality of the visible world gives one the impression that it exists for ends beyond itself; those ends are eternal and so the world is eternal.

The king, being wise, will take a lesson from this. To be first among men, he must be last in his own calculations; and if he is last, he will be first. His salvation is in self-denial. He will find fulfillment as a man and king in being selfless.

8

The highest goodness, water-like,
Does good to everything and goes
Unmurmuring to places men despise;
But so, is close in nature to the Way.

If the good of the house is from land,
Or the good of the mind is its depth,
Or love is the virtue of friendship,
Or honesty blesses one's talk,
Or in government, goodness is order,
Or in business, skill is admired,
Or the worth of an act lies in timing,
Then peace is the goal of the Way
By which no one ever goes astray.

PARAPHRASE

The highest goodness, like water, is characterized by humility. A good man or a good king is self-effacing like the Way.

Consequently, his object is peace; and the picture of peace consists of families secure on their land and the people thoughtful, kind and honest. It also requires orderly government and skillful business, with the king doing what is his to do at the appropriate times.

Comment: This poem is supplemented by Poem 80, *q.v.*

9

To take all you want
Is never as good
As to stop when you should.
Scheme and be sharp
And you'll not keep it long.
One never can guard
His home when it's full
Of jade and fine gold:
Wealth, power and pride
Bequeath their own doom.
When fame and success
Come to you, then retire.
This is the ordained Way.

COMMENT

One can only guess that this bitter reproach was addressed to the nobility and palace sycophants. It could hardly have been aimed at the king, for it would have destroyed the illusion that he is the "Wise Man." Imperial politics in the last centuries of the Chou dynasty was like placer mining: when the operation was finished, all the nuggets were extracted from the gravel.

10

Can you govern your animal soul, hold to the One
and never depart from it?
Can you throttle your breath, down to the softness of
breath in a child?
Can you purify your mystic vision and wash it until it
is spotless?
Can you love all your people, rule over the land without being known?
Can you be like a female, and passively open and shut
heaven's gates?
Can you keep clear in your mind the four quarters of
earth and not interfere?

Quicken them, feed them;
Quicken but do not possess them.
Act and be independent;
Be the chief but never the lord:
This describes the mystic virtue.

PARAPHRASE

Can you control your animal nature enough to be
pure in heart, never distracted from the one Way?
Are you capable of the personal disciplines that can
enable you to love unselfishly, wield virtue and at last
understand all, while denying yourself?

Put life into your people without trying to own
them. Depend on no one. Be their king but never the
tyrant. This is what our mysticism requires of you.

Comment: This poem contains the single reference
to native yoga. (See Introduction.)

11

Thirty spokes will converge
In the hub of a wheel;
But the use of the cart
Will depend on the part
Of the hub that is void.

With a wall all around
A clay bowl is molded;
But the use of the bowl
Will depend on the part
Of the bowl that is void.

Cut out windows and doors
In the house as you build;
But the use of the house
Will depend on the space
In the walls that is void.

So advantage is had
From whatever is there;
But usefulness rises
From whatever is not.

PARAPHRASE

Is the Way real? Does it exist? Can one isolate it and say, "This is it"? It is as real as the hole in the hub of a wheel where the axle rests. The hole is a void in the hub. It exists as a window exists when part of the wall of a house is cut away. Similarly, the Way is like the empty place in a bowl. The advantage of a bowl lies in its walls but its use depends on its emptiness. So with the Way. It is functional. It cannot be isolated, but you cannot be without it.

12

The five colors darken the eye;
The five sounds will deaden the ear;
The five flavors weary the taste;
Chasing the beasts of the field
Will drive a man mad.
The goods that are hard to procure
Are hobbles that slow walking feet.

So the Wise Man will do
What his belly dictates
And never the sight of his eyes.
Thus he will choose this but not that.

PARAPHRASE

Beware of sensual enjoyment and of the pretty things that surround the king to seduce him from his real calling. The usual pursuits of the nobles and the luxury of the palaces will ruin the king.

The king, therefore, should follow his inward, private feelings about things; let him not be deluded by what his senses report. He must discriminate, selecting some things as admissible and others as undesirable.

13

"Favor, like disgrace
Brings trouble with it;
High rank, like self,
Involves acute distress."

What does that mean, to say
That "favor, like disgrace
Brings trouble with it"?
When favor is bestowed
On one of low degree,

Trouble will come with it.
The loss of favor too
Means trouble for that man.
This, then, is what is meant
By "favor, like disgrace
Brings trouble with it."

What does it mean, to say
That "rank, like self,
Involves acute distress"?
I suffer most because
Of me and selfishness.
If I were selfless, then
What suffering would I bear?

In governing the world,
Let rule entrusted be
To him who treats his rank
As if it were his soul;
World sovereignty can be
Committed to that man
Who loves all people
As he loves himself.

PARAPHRASE

If high rank comes to one or leaves him, he will suffer for the egotism involved. Only those to whom high rank is a great trust and who love people are fit for government.

14

They call it elusive, and say
That one looks
But it never appears.
They say that indeed it is rare,
Since one listens,
But never a sound.
Subtle, they call it, and say
That one grasps it
But never gets hold.
These three complaints amount
To only one, which is
Beyond all resolution.

At rising, it does not illumine;
At setting, no darkness ensues;
It stretches far back
To that nameless estate
Which existed before the creation.

Describe it as form yet unformed;
As shape that is still without shape;
Or say it is vagueness confused:
One meets it and it has no front;
One follows and there is no rear.

If you hold ever fast
To that most ancient Way,
You may govern today.
Call truly that knowledge
Of primal beginnings
The clue to the Way.

PARAPHRASE

The Way is invisible, inaudible, intangible and must be accepted as such. Its presence can never be put to a definite test, so that being present, it gives no light; being absent, it leaves no darkness. It meets no human specifications.

Let the king be ever mindful of it. It is the first fact of the world, without which present government would be impossible. Study the way of the ancient rulers; what they did is your clue today.

15

The excellent masters of old,
Subtle, mysterious, mystic, acute,
Were much too profound for their times.
Since they were not then understood,
It is better to tell how they looked.

Like men crossing streams in the winter,
    How cautious!
As if all around there were danger,
    How watchful!
As if they were guests on every occasion,
    How dignified!
Like ice just beginning to melt,
    Self-effacing!
Like a wood-block untouched by a tool,
    How sincere!
Like a valley awaiting a guest,
    How receptive!
Like a torrent that rushes along,
    And so turbid!

Who, running dirty, comes clean like still waters?
Who, being quiet, moves others to fullness of life?
It is he who, embracing the Way, is not greedy;
Who endures wear and tear without needing renewal.

PARAPHRASE

The king should look the part of the Wise Man
who, in turn, follows the attitudes and manners of ancient kings. Here is the prescription; it is selected for
authenticity from classic sources and presented in the
approved form. It answers the question most characteristic of the age: according to your idea, what would your
ideal man look like as he went about his business?

16

Touch ultimate emptiness,
Hold steady and still.

All things work together:
I have watched them reverting,
And have seen how they flourish
And return again, each to his roots.

This, I say, is the stillness:
A retreat to one's roots;
Or better yet, return
To the will of God,
Which is, I say, to constancy.
The knowledge of constancy
I call enlightenment and say
That not to know it
Is blindness that works evil.

But when you know
What eternally is so,
You have stature
And stature means righteousness
And righteousness is kingly
And kingliness divine
And divinity is the Way
Which is final.

Then, though you die,
You shall not perish.

PARAPHRASE

Deep in all there is a stillness, where the root of
life is, and the root is God, from whom destiny proceeds, and without knowledge of that root, the eternal
root, a man is blind and will therefore work evil. Let
the king take note.

When he knows that root, he will be of great stature

as a man and king whose righteousness endows him
with kingliness and makes him at last divine because
the Way is at work in him. Thus, the king may die
but he will not perish.

17

As for him who is highest,
The people just know he is there.
His deputy's cherished and praised;
Of the third, they are frightened;
The fourth, they despise and revile.
If you trust people less than enough,
Some of them never trust you.

He is aloof, as if his talk
Were priced beyond the purchasing;
But once his project is contrived,
The folk will want to say of it:
"Of course! We did it by ourselves!"

PARAPHRASE

In the hierarchy of government, the king is only a name to the people; his deputy is loved and praised because the people want to have faith in someone high in government; the third in command is more familiar but still out of reach and so he is feared; the man in the fourth grade down from majesty is on the firing line and will be the target for all who are vexed.

But the king is aloof and the people never hear his voice. If he succeeds in embodying the Way in his government, all the people could desire will come to pass and they will never know that it was not their own achievement.

18

The mighty Way declined among the folk
And then came kindness and morality.
When wisdom and intelligence appeared,
They brought with them a great hypocrisy.
The six relations were no more at peace,
So codes were made to regulate our homes.
The fatherland grew dark, confused by strife:
Official loyalty became the style.

PARAPHRASE

There was a time when men shared with all other
creatures the balance of nature, its spontaneity and
effortless change. Then the process of civilization set
in with its inevitable constituents, kindness, morality,
wisdom and intelligence. Their opposites came with
them (2), unkindness, immorality, foolishness and stupidity. Then there was trouble everywhere. The six
family relations (father and son, elder and younger
brothers, husband and wife) are disturbed. The loyalty
of public officers has become a pretense.

Comment: The thought of this poem is extended in
Poem 19. It is restated in Poem 38.

19

Get rid of the wise men!
Put out the professors!
Then people will profit
A hundredfold over.
Away with the kind ones;
Those righteous men too!
And let people return
To the graces of home.
Root out the artisans;
Banish the profiteers!
And bandits and robbers
Will not come to plunder.

But if these three prove not enough
To satisfy the mind and heart,
More relevant, then, let there be
A visible simplicity of life,
Embracing unpretentious ways,
And small self-interest
And poverty of coveting.

COMMENT

Obviously, in the latter part of the Chou era, there were too many professors of theories designed to mend the evil times. Their disputes bred confusion. It would be better, says the writer, to do away with them all (including the writer?) and rely on the goodness and wisdom of the people themselves.

This poem is a redaction of a passage in Chuang Chou (chap. 10) which makes it clear that the protest is against the professors and not against wisdom. He specifies, for example, that two Confucian scholars, Tseng and Shih, should be severely restrained and that even Yang Chu and Mo Ti should be gagged, so that the people could be moral without hindrance!

20

Be done with rote learning
And its attendant vexations;
For is there distinction
Of a "yes" from a "yea"
Comparable now to the gulf
Between evil and good?
"What all men fear, I too must fear"—
How barren and pointless a thought!

The reveling of multitudes
At the feast of Great Sacrifice,
Or up on the terrace
At carnival in spring,
Leave me, alas, unmoved, alone,
Like a child that has never smiled.

Lazily, I drift
As though I had no home.
All others have enough to spare;
I am the one left out.
I have the mind of a fool,
Muddled and confused!
When common people scintillate
I alone make shadows.
Vulgar folks are sharp and knowing:
Only I am melancholy.
Restless like the ocean,
Blown about, I cannot stop.
Other men can find employment,
But I am stubborn; I am mean.

Alone I am and different,
Because I prize and seek
My sustenance from the Mother!

COMMENT

The first stanza above is a protest against the learning of catechisms required of those who aspire to court life, where the difference between "yes" and "yea" is made to seem as important as the difference between good and evil.

21

The omnipresent Virtue will take shape
According only to the Way.
The Way itself is like some thing
Seen in a dream, elusive, evading one.
In it are images, elusive, evading one.
In it are things like shadows in twilight.
In it are essences, subtle but real,
Embedded in truth.

From of old until now,
Under names without end,
The First, the Beginning is seen.
How do I know the beginning of all,
What its nature may be?
By these!

PARAPHRASE

There is a virtue, a power that issues from the Way
like a magnetic field around a magnet. As the magnet
controls the shape of the field, so the Way controls its
virtue or power.

The Way itself is impalpable, immaterial, and yet
out of it are the issues of life.

From ancient times until now, the Beginning, the
Way, has been presented under an endless number of
names. How may I know what it is? By what I have
told about, my insights, my intuitions, my experience
with what is eternal, always so.

22

The crooked shall be made straight
And the rough places plain;
The pools shall be filled
And the worn renewed;
The needy shall receive
And the rich shall be perplexed.

So the Wise Man cherishes the One,
As a standard to the world:
Not displaying himself,
He is famous;
Not asserting himself,
He is distinguished;
Not boasting his powers,
He is effective;
Taking no pride in himself,
He is chief.

Because he is no competitor,
No one in all the world
Can compete with him.

The saying of the men of old
Is not in vain:
"The crooked shall be made straight—"
To be perfect, return to it.

PARAPHRASE

In words suggestive of the Hebrew prophets, the writer says that the Way, like Jahweh, is the restorer and mender of inequities. This thought should prove attractive to the ruler of distressed people.

Let the king therefore embrace the One, the Way, by his own quietness (inaction), and then, through him, the Way will take care of the needs of all.

Comment: This poem indicates that civilized society is contemplated as a result of the Way's virtue. The king would still be king and the wrongs of society righted.

23

Sparing indeed is nature of its talk:
The whirlwind will not last the morning out;
The cloudburst ends before the day is done.
What is it that behaves itself like this?
The earth and sky! And if it be that these
Cut short their speech, how much more yet should man!

If you work by the Way,
You will be of the Way;
If you work through its virtue
You will be given the virtue;
Abandon either one
And both abandon you.

Gladly then the Way receives
Those who choose to walk in it;
Gladly too its power upholds
Those who choose to use it well;
Gladly will abandon greet
Those who to abandon drift.

Little faith is put in them
Whose faith is small.

PARAPHRASE

"In the multitude of words there wanteth not sin:
but he that refraineth his lips is wise." (Proverbs
10:19.)

If the people are to put faith in the king, his faith
in the Way must be great. His hope for success lies in
the Way and its power; if he were once to abandon
it, he himself would be abandoned indeed.

24

On tiptoe your stance is unsteady;
Long strides make your progress unsure;
Show off and you get no attention;
Your boasting will mean you have failed;
Asserting yourself brings no credit;
Be proud and you never will lead.

To persons of the Way, these traits
Can only bring distrust; they seem
Like extra food for parasites.
So those who choose the Way,
Will never give them place.

PARAPHRASE

The king will avoid temptations to stand "on tiptoe," i.e., to ambition, special advantages, exhibition-
ism, boasting, dictatorship and pride.

There are always some persons around who, since
they are on the Way, will see these traits and be dis-
gusted by them. To such people they will be like the
surplus food, the poor food, prepared by a family to
feed unwelcome human parasites, who attach themselves to the family on more or less public occasions,
when to refuse them food would bring adverse comment from the guests.

25

Something there is, whose veiled creation was
Before the earth or sky began to be;
So silent, so aloof and so alone,
It changes not, nor fails, but touches all:
Conceive it as the mother of the world.

I do not know its name;
A name for it is "Way";
Pressed for designation,
I call it Great.
Great means outgoing,
Outgoing, far-reaching,
Far-reaching, return.

The Way is great,
The sky is great,
The earth is great,
The king also is great.
Within the realm
These four are great;
The king but stands
For one of them.

Man conforms to the earth;
The earth conforms to the sky;
The sky conforms to the Way;
The Way conforms to its own nature.

PARAPHRASE

The first two stanzas are a restatement of the argument of Poem 1. The Way is really nameless; it is not a phenomenon, but the description in the second stanza once again suggests the lines of force in a magnetic field. They go out from one pole and return to the other.

Everything in the universe takes its greatness from the Way, and of this, the king is the human symbol. He is the Man who, through the earth and the heavens, connects all of us with the Way.

26

The heavy is foundation for the light;
So quietness is master of the deed.

The Wise Man, though he travel all the day,
Will not be separated from his goods.
So even if the scene is glorious to view,
He keeps his place, at peace, above it all.

For how can one who rules
Ten thousand chariots
Give up to lighter moods
As all the world may do?
If he is trivial,
His ministers are lost;
If he is strenuous,
There is no master then.

PARAPHRASE

The people who are light of fancy must have a master who is not easily moved. The king should never allow himself to be distracted from his mission. He is not free to relax his attention from affairs of state as other people are. Most important, he must be quiet, unmoved, if he is to be master of those who do the governing.

The "chariots" were the ancient equivalent of modern army tanks. Ten thousand chariots would indicate formidable military power.

27

A good runner leaves no tracks.

A good speech has no flaws to censure.

A good computer uses no tallies.

A good door is well shut without bolts and cannot be opened.

A good knot is tied without rope and cannot be loosed.

The Wise Man is always good at helping people, so that none are cast out; he is always good at saving things, so that none are thrown away. This is called applied intelligence.

Surely the good man is the bad man's teacher; and the bad man is the good man's business. If the one does not respect his teacher, or the other doesn't love his business, his error is very great.

This is indeed an important secret.

COMMENT

This chapter is developed from epigrams and is not poetry. The epigrams more or less suggestively describe the Wise Man. The symbolism of the door is familiar to readers of the New Testament: "I am the door"; "and the door was shut." So are the remaining portions.

28

Be aware of your masculine nature;
But by keeping the feminine way,
You shall be to the world like a canyon,
Where the Virtue eternal abides,
And go back to become as a child.

Be aware of the white all around you;
But rememb'ring the black that is there,
You shall be to the world like a tester,
Whom the Virtue eternal, unerring,
Redirects to the infinite past.

Be aware of your glory and honor;
But in never relinquishing shame,
You shall be to the world like a valley,
Where Virtue eternal, sufficient,
Sends you back to the Virginal Block.

When the Virginal Block is asunder,
And is made into several tools,
To the ends of the Wise Man directed,
They become then his chief officers:
For "The Master himself does not carve."

PARAPHRASE

You are masculine; but if the Way is to work
through you, you must be passive, as if feminine. This
takes practice and in the end you will be rewarded
with childlikeness. The Virtue of the Way will come
into you when you are empty like a valley or canyon,
and therefore receptive to it. You will then be sensitive equally to good and bad as they concern you and
will be able to test everything for its worth; in the end
you will come to terms with the effortless worth that
is located in the distant past.

You will take glory in your stride but keep your
shame too; in the end you will be like the valley which

is the favorite resort of the Way and its Virtue. You will there revert to "the Virginal Block," the primal simplicity. When the king has men who are fresh as children are, he can make good officials out of them. This is his skill.

29

As for those who would take the whole world
To tinker it as they see fit,
I observe that they never succeed:
For the world is a sacred vessel
Not made to be altered by man.
The tinker will spoil it;
Usurpers will lose it.

For indeed there are things
That must move ahead,
While others must lag;
And some that feel hot,
While others feel cold;
And some that are strong,
While others are weak;
And vigorous ones,
With others worn out.

So the Wise Man discards
Extreme inclinations
To make sweeping judgments,
Or to a life of excess.

PARAPHRASE

The world is not to be owned and tinkered by any man; it belongs to God and those who try to usurp his right will fail.

Things generally have their own individual characteristics and cannot be made to submit to the whims of one person.

The king, therefore, will avoid the temptation to try to make everything in the world conform to his plan and serve his vanity.

30

To those who would help
The ruler of men
By means of the Way:

Let him not with his militant might
Try to conquer the world;
This tactic is like to recoil.
For where armies have marched,
There do briars spring up;
Where great hosts are impressed,
Years of hunger and evil ensue.

The good man's purpose once attained,
He stops at that;
He will not press for victory.
His point once made, he does not boast,
Or celebrate the goal he gained,
Or proudly indicate the spoils.
He won the day because he must:
But not by force or violence.

That things with age decline in strength,
You well may say, suits not the Way;
And not to suit the Way is early death.

COMMENT

One can only conjecture the identity of the "ruler
of men," and his counsellors: are they the king of
Ch'in and the Legalists? (Introduction, pp. 25–27.)
Post hoc, their tactics did recoil. The poem is, however, quite general and generally justified.

31

Weapons at best are tools of bad omen,
Loathed and avoided by those of the Way.

In the usage of men of good breeding,
Honor is had at the left;
Good omens belong on the left;
Bad omens belong on the right;
And warriors press to the right!
When the general stands at the right
His lieutenant is placed at the left.
So the usage of men of great power
Follows that of the funeral rite.

Weapons are tools of bad omen,
By gentlemen not to be used;
But when it cannot be avoided,
They use them with calm and restraint.
Even in victory's hour
These tools are unlovely to see;
For those who admire them truly
Are men who in murder delight.

As for those who delight to do murder,
It is certain they never can get
From the world what they sought when ambition
Urged them to power and rule.

A multitude slain!—and their death
Is a matter for grief and for tears;
The victory after a conflict
Is a theme for a funeral rite.

COMMENT

I have rearranged the material of this chapter in
view of the well-known, confusing interpolations. It

reflects bitter experience with internecine strife. Slyly, it compares the protocol of military life with that of funerals. Even when a soldier is successful, his success is a matter for grief.

第三十二章

道常無名朴雖小天下不敢臣侯王

若能守萬物將自賓天地相合以降

甘露民莫之令而自均始制有名名

亦既有夫亦將知止知止所以不殆

譬道之在天下猶川谷之於江海也

The text, in Chinese, of the poem on the following page.

32

The Way eternal has no name.
A block of wood untooled, though small,
May still excel the world.
And if the king and nobles could
Retain its potency for good,
Then everything would freely give
Allegiance to their rule.

The earth and sky would then conspire
To bring the sweet dew down;
And evenly it would be given
To folk without constraining power.

Creatures came to be with order's birth,
And once they had appeared,
Came also knowledge of repose,
And with that was security.

In this world,
Compare those of the Way
To torrents that flow
Into river and sea.

PARAPHRASE

The Way, by nature, is *sui generis,* unique, and there
is no name that applies to it. The bit of untouched
substance, symbolized by the Virgin Block of wood,
has untold possibilities in it; whereas the world is limited because it is an accomplished fact. If the king and
nobles could hold on to the possibilities for good in
what they control, they could rule the world, and
heaven and earth would conspire to bring down peace
for all people alike.

From the beginning of the ordered world, the possi-
bility of repose made all creatures secure.

33

It is wisdom to know others;
It is enlightenment to know one's self.

The conqueror of men is powerful;
The master of himself is strong.

It is wealth to be content;
It is willful to force one's way on others.

Endurance is to keep one's place;
Long life it is to die and not perish.

COMMENT

These couplets are not plucked bits of popular wisdom. They are constructed by the mystic in praise of self-knowledge, self-mastery, quietude and acceptance of one's place in the scheme of nature.

The Way gives life and the Way gives death: who will object? Certainly not one who knows himself, or is master of himself, or who has learned contentment. Such a person knows his place in nature and keeps it. He accepts death as he accepts life and, accordingly, does not perish; for he belongs to the eternal scheme of things. Of sentient creatures, it is only man who needs to learn this wisdom.

34

O the great Way o'erflows
And spreads on every side!
All being comes from it;
No creature is denied.
But having called them forth,
It calls not one its own.
It feeds and clothes them all
And will not be their lord.

Without desire always,
It seems of slight import.
Yet, nonetheless, in this
Its greatness still appears:
When they return to it,
No creature meets a lord,

The Wise Man, therefore, while he is alive,
Will never make a show of being great:
And that is how his greatness is achieved.

PARAPHRASE

It is characteristic of the Way that, while it is everywhere, in everything, giving life to all, it is never coercive or possessive. The Way is without desire, and yet, this is the measure of its greatness. It is also the measure of greatness of the Wise Man, the king, who conforms to it.

35

Once grasp the great Form without form,
And you roam where you will
With no evil to fear,
Calm, peaceful, at ease.

At music and viands
The wayfarer stops.
But the Way, when declared,
Seems thin and so flavorless!

It is nothing to look at
And nothing to hear;
But used, it will prove
Inexhaustible.

COMMENT

The "Form without form" suggests the Platonic form or idea, an archetype; it is the all-embracing form or idea in which things exist potentially until realized in the actual world.

36

What is to be shrunken
Is first stretched out;
What is to be weakened
Is first made strong;
What will be thrown over
Is first raised up;
What will be withdrawn
Is first bestowed.

This indeed is
Subtle Light;
The gentle way
Will overcome
The hard and strong.
As fish should not
Get out of pools,
The realm's edged tools
Should not be shown
To anybody.

PARAPHRASE

Lest the king misunderstand his present strength,
let him know that it is a common lot among men and
kings to be built up for a fall. So Han Fei (d. 233 B.C.),
at least, interprets the first stanza.

A subtler understanding, however, should make the
king aware that gentleness is stronger than harshness.

In any case, let the king not advertise himself or his
powers. As fish should not get out of pools, the wise
men, "the edged tools" of the realm, should keep out
of sight. The king is the Wise Man. The metaphor of
the last five lines is adapted from *Chuang Tzu*
(chap. 10).

37

The Way is always still, at rest,
And yet does everything that's done.
If then the king and nobles could
Retain its potency for good,
The creatures all would be transformed.

But if, the change once made in them,
They still inclined to do their work,
I should restrain them then
By means of that unique
Original simplicity
Found in the Virgin Block,
Which brings disinterest,
With stillness in its train,
And so, an ordered world.

PARAPHRASE

The Way accomplishes everything that happens
without itself doing anything (*Wei wu wei*). It is the
unmoved mover. If, as in Poem 32, the king and nobles could rest in the Way, without interfering in anything, the world they govern would be a very
different place.

But if, when the Way had done its work in all
things, they still showed restlessness, I should apply
the principle of which the Virgin Block is a symbol
and stop the process. There is a natural simplicity
which obtained in the world under the first rulers, Yao
and Shun, when the virtues of disinterest, stillness and
order were achieved. This is the goal.

38

A man of highest virtue
Will not display it as his own;
His virtue then is real.
Low virtue makes one miss no chance
To show his virtue off;
His virtue then is nought.
High virtue is at rest;
It knows no need to act.
Low virtue is a busyness
Pretending to accomplishment.

Compassion at its best
Consists in honest deeds;
Morality at best
Is something done, aforethought;
High etiquette, when acted out
Without response from others,
Constrains a man to bare his arms
And make them do their duty!

Truly, once the Way is lost,
There comes then virtue;
Virtue lost, comes then compassion;
After that morality;
And when that's lost, there's etiquette,
The husk of all good faith,
The rising point of anarchy.

Foreknowledge is, they say,
The Doctrine* come to flower;
But better yet, it is
The starting point of stillness.

---

*I.e., Confucian doctrine, the ascendant orthodoxy. See *Analects* II:23, "Whatever others may succeed the Chou, their character, even a hundred ages hence, can be known."

So once full-grown, a man will take
The meat and not the husk,
The fruit and not the flower.
Rejecting one, he takes the other.

39

These things in ancient times received the One:

The sky obtained it and was clarified;
The earth received it and was settled firm;
The spirits got it and were energized;
The valleys had it, filled to overflow;
All things, as they partook it came alive;
The nobles and the king imbibed the One
In order that the realm might upright be;
Such things were then accomplished by the One.

Without its clarity the sky might break;
Except it were set firm, the earth might shake;
Without their energy the gods would pass;
Unless kept full, the valleys might go dry;
Except for life, all things would pass away;
Unless the One did lift and hold them high,
The nobles and the king might trip and fall.

The humble folk support the mighty ones;
They are base on which the highest rest.
The nobles and the king speak of themselves
As "orphans," "desolate" and "needy ones."
Does this not indicate that they depend
Upon the lowly people for support?

Truly, a cart is more than the sum of its parts.

Better to rumble like rocks
Than to tinkle like jade.

COMMENT

The use of "the One" as a synonym for the Way
indicates the unifying character of the Way. This poem
is an assertion that the Way is immanent everywhere.

40

The movement of the Way is a return;
In weakness lies its major usefulness.
From What-is all the world of things was born
But What-is sprang in turn from What-is-not.

COMMENT

The first line simply reasserts Poem 25, line 12, or the first part of Poem 16. It is worth noting that while Chinese custom set the Golden Age in the past, this "return" does not necessarily mean going back by imitating the primitive ancients. The mystic in China, as elsewhere, was interested in exploring the roots as well as the fruits of life, in an effort to know the ultimate truth about himself and everything else. It is rather a return to "within" one's self, where the ultimate mystery of being can eventually be confronted.

The "weakness" of the Way is like the "weakness" of Jesus on trial. Poem 8, line 1, however, describes the highest goodness as being like water. Poem 76, line 11: "The soft and yielding rise above them all."

"What-is," or being, is the "mother" or matrix of Poem 1, line 4. "What-is-not," or nonbeing, is described more at length in Poem 4, lines 1–5. It is the Way, the "preface to God."

41

On hearing of the Way, the best of men
Will earnestly explore its length.
The mediocre person learns of it
And takes it up and sets it down.
But vulgar people, when they hear the news,
Will laugh out loud, and if they did not laugh,
It would not be the Way.

And so there is a proverb:
"When going looks like coming back,
The clearest road is mighty dark."
     Today, the Way that's plain looks rough,
     And lofty virtue like a chasm;
     The purest innocence like shame,
     The broadest power not enough,
     Established goodness knavery,
     Substantial worth like shifting tides.

Great space has no corners;
Great powers come late;
Great music is soft sound;
The great Form no shape.

The Way is obscure and unnamed;
It is a skilled investor, nonetheless,
The master of accomplishment.

PARALLELS

"Many are called but few are chosen." (Matthew 22:14)

"Darkness shall cover the earth, and gross darkness
the people." (Isaiah 60:2)

"To whom then will you liken me, or shall I be equal?"
(Isaiah 40:25)

"Yet he gave to as many as took him
The power to be Children of God." (John 1:12)

42

The Way begot one,
And the one, two;
Then the two begot three
And three, all else.

All things bear the shade on their backs
And the sun in their arms;
By the blending of breath
From the sun and the shade,
Equilibrium comes to the world.

Orphaned, or needy, or desolate, these
Are conditions much feared and disliked;
Yet in public address, the king
And the nobles account themselves thus.
So a loss sometimes benefits one
Or a benefit proves to be loss.

What others have taught
I also shall teach:
If a violent man does not come
To a violent death,
I shall choose him to teach me.

COMMENT

There is a passage in *Chuang Tzu* (chap. 2) from
which the first stanza is adapted: "The world and I
have a common origin and all creatures and I together
are one. Being one, our oneness can be expressed . . .
or unexpressed. The one, with the expression, makes
two, and the two, with one (what is unexpressed),
make three. From there on. . . ." Here is a triad: the
world of things, what can be said of it, and what cannot be said of it.

The second stanza introduces the Yin-Yang cognates as shade and sun, their "breaths" being cold or warm. The third stanza is a play on the conventional speech of royalty. The fourth stanza may refer to one of Mo Ti's approved doctrines: violence is evil.

43

The softest of stuff in the world
Penetrates quickly the hardest;
Insubstantial, it enters
Where no room is.

By this I know the benefit
Of something done by quiet being;
In all the world but few can know
Accomplishment apart from work,
Instruction when no words are used.

PARAPHRASE

On the analogy of water, the softest stuff, penetrating rocks, the insubstantial Way gets into everything, even when it seems that there is no place for it.

Yet neither water nor the Way attempts this penetration; it happens without effort, without *doing* on the part of the Way or resistance on the part of whatever is penetrated. The creature simply gives up to its Creator.

44

Which is dearer, fame or self?
Which is worth more, man or pelf?
Which would hurt more, gain or loss?

The mean man pays the highest price;
The hoarder takes the greatest loss;
A man content is never shamed,
And self-restrained, is not in danger:
He will live forever.

COMMENT

There is a neat symmetry about this piece. The
mean man pays the highest price because he trades
virtue for gain. The hoarder takes the greatest loss
because he accumulates pelf in preference to virtue.
The "man content" has virtue and is self-restrained
and so is never in danger from shame or death.

45

Most perfect, yet it seems
Imperfect, incomplete:
Its use is not impaired.
Filled up, and yet it seems
Poured out, an empty void:
It never will run dry.

The straightest, yet it seems
To deviate, to bend;
The highest skill and yet
It looks like clumsiness.
The utmost eloquence,
It sounds like stammering.*

As movement overcomes
The cold, and stillness, heat,
The Wise Man, pure and still,
Will rectify the world.

PARAPHRASE

The Way, unnamed, though ideal for every good purpose, seems to ordinary observers both defective and stupid. Nevertheless, by means of it, the king can bring order and probity to the world.

Comment: In this poem, as in others in this collection, the thought is paradoxical, but the paradox asserts the contrast between appearance and reality: the commonsense judgments of men rest on appearances and are contradicted by reality. This point of view is parallel to that of the *Divine Comedy* of Dante, or the gospel: God and man do not always see eye to eye: what God makes perfect may seem imperfect to

---

*See *Exodus* 4:10, "Moses said . . . 'but I am slow of speech, and of a slow tongue.'" Also see *Analects* IV:24, "The aristocrat likes to be slow of speech and prompt to act."

the human observer, and vice versa. Paradox is generally characteristic of mystic writing, from which drama and high comedy are seldom missing. Indeed, the paradox of the mystic is really germinal drama that fired the imaginations of China's artists and writers.

46

When the Way rules the world,
Coach horses fertilize fields;
When the Way does not rule,
War horses breed in the parks.

No sin can exceed
Incitement to envy;
No calamity's worse
Than to be discontented,
Nor is there an omen
More dreadful than coveting.
But once be contented,
And truly you'll always be so.

PARAPHRASE

When the Way prevails, nobody wants to go any-
where and the coach horses are turned out to pasture;
when the Way does not prevail, cavalry horses are
bred in the city parks.

The Wise Man, the king, should be contented. With
what? The only permanent contentment is that of nature: it is contented to be contented.

47

The world may be known
Without leaving the house;
The Way may be seen
Apart from the windows.
The further you go,
The less you will know.

Accordingly, the Wise Man
Knows without going,
Sees without seeing,
Does without doing.

PARAPHRASE

The inner world of a man reflects the world around him; the principles of both worlds are the same. Certainty is to be found only in the heart; confusion is bred in the outer world.

48

The student learns by daily increment.
The Way is gained by daily loss,
Loss upon loss until
At last comes rest.

By letting go, it all gets done;
The world is won by those who let it go!
But when you try and try,
The world is then beyond the winning.

PARAPHRASE

A student adds each day to his stock of knowledge
or experience; but the attainment of the Way is not
like that. Each day one sheds a selfish impulse or desire and continues to do so until his will is at rest in
the Way and is undistracted.

One can let go of everything except the Way; but
having the Way, one has the whole world with it. The
world can be mine if I do not try to own it or run it
according to my ideas. When I do try to run it, then
I lose it altogether. Let the king be well advised that
he can have everything he does not try to possess
selfishly.

49

The Wise Man's mind is free
But tuned to people's need:
  "Alike to good and bad
  I must be good,
  For Virtue is goodness.
  To honest folk
  And those dishonest ones
  Alike, I proffer faith,
  For Virtue is faithful."

The Wise Man, when abroad,
Impartial to the world,
Does not divide or judge.
But people everywhere
Mark well his ears and eyes;
For wise men hear and see
As little children do.

COMMENT

This poem represents the Wise Man as disinterested, objective in his view of people. He will not be a "judge or divider" over them. He will cause "his sun to rise on the evil and the good" and send "rain on the just and unjust." This poem has caused some commentators to say the mystics are morally indifferent. Quite to the contrary, their virtue is more than social convention; it is a property of the Way and as I have indicated in the Introduction it is moral.

Scholarly critics have tinkered with lines five and nine in verse one above to make them read "and so I obtain goodness," "and so I obtain good faith." With those who prefer these readings I shall not quarrel.

50

On leaving life, to enter death:
Thirteen members form a living body;
A corpse has thirteen, too:
Thirteen spots by which a man may pass
From life to death. Why so?
Because his way of life
Is much too gross.

As I have heard, the man who knows
On land how best to be at peace
Will never meet a tiger or a buffalo;
In battle, weapons do not touch his skin.
There is no place the tiger's claws can grip;
Or with his horn, the buffalo can jab;
Or where the soldier can insert his sword.
Why so? In him there is no place of death.

PARAPHRASE

A man has thirteen vital organs through which death may come to him. By ancient lore, there are "the four limbs and the nine external cavities." These spots of danger circumvent his will to live.

The Wise Man, however, is in no danger. His thirteen organs have nothing to do with his life or death. He lives by the Way.

The legend was that Socrates was similarly invulnerable.

51

The Way brings forth,
Its Virtue fosters them,
With matter they take shape,
And circumstance perfects them all:
    That is why all things
    Do honor to the Way
    And venerate its power.

The exaltation of the Way,
The veneration of its power,
Come not by fate or by decree;
But always just because
By nature it is so.

So when the Way brings forth,
Its power fosters all:
They grow, are reared,
And fed and housed until
They come to ripe maturity.
    You shall give life to things
    But never possess them;
    Your work shall depend on none;
    You shall be chief but never lord.

This describes the mystic power.

COMMENT

This hymn connects the Way with the king or, for
that matter, anyone. This I have indicated by the addition of the words, "you shall," in lines 18–21. The last
five lines are identical in the Chinese with the last five
lines of Poem 10, *q.v.*

52

It began with a matrix:
The world had a mother
Whose sons can be known
As ever, by her.
But if you know them,
You'll keep close to her
As long as you live
And suffer no harm.

Stop up your senses;
Close up your doors;
Be not exhausted
As long as you live.
Open your senses;
Be busier still:
To the end of your days
There's no help for you.

You are bright, it is said,
If you see what is small;
A store of small strengths
Makes you strong.
By the use of its light,
Make your eyes again bright
From evil to lead you away.

This is called "practicing constancy."

PARAPHRASE

The closer you keep to the "mother," begotten by the Way, that is to say, to the beginning of the world, the safer you will be.

Live within yourself; do not exhaust yourself in the world as it is.

Your perspicacity grows by small increments, so they say, but only by trusting the light of the Way can true intelligence come to you.

53

When I am walking on the mighty Way,
Let me but know the very least I may,
And I shall only fear to leave the road.
The mighty Way is easy underfoot,
But people still prefer the little paths.

The royal court is dignified, sedate,
While farmers' fields are overgrown with weeds;
The granaries are empty and yet they
Are clad in rich-embroidered silken gowns.
They have sharp swords suspended at their sides;
With glutted wealth, they gorge with food and drink.

It is, the people say,
The boastfulness of brigandage,
But surely not the Way!

PARAPHRASE

No matter how ignorant I may be, at least I know
better than to get off the Way. It is a smooth Way;
and yet people, especially the people around the king,
prefer the bypaths of sensuality.

Meanwhile, the people fare badly; robbed by the
nobles, they have no strength left to tend their farms.

The people are saying that the king is surrounded
by loud bandits.

54

Set firm in the Way: none shall uproot you;
Cherish it well and none shall estrange you;
Your children's children faithful shall serve
Your forebears at the altar of your house.

Cultivate the Way yourself,
    and your Virtue will be genuine.
Cultivate it in the home,
    and its Virtue will overflow.
Cultivate it in the village,
    and the village will endure.
Cultivate it in the realm,
    and the realm will flourish.
Cultivate it in the world,
    and Virtue will be universal.

Accordingly,
    One will be judged by the Man of the Way;
    Homes will be viewed through the Home of the Way;
    And the Village shall measure the village;
    And the Realm, for all realms, shall be standard;
    And the World, to this world, shall be heaven.

How do I know the world is like this?
By this.

PARAPHRASE

Everything depends on man's relation to the Way,
especially the form of virtue appropriate to each field
of interest and endeavor.

This leads to the consideration of the ideal person,
home, village, realm or world. The actual man is the
avenue through which the ideal Man is contemplated.

But once a man is set firm in the Way, he becomes the ideal and the standard by which all actual men are judged.

I know this by intuition.

55

Rich in virtue, like an infant,
Noxious insects will not sting him;
Wild beasts will not attack his flesh
Nor birds of prey sink claws in him.

His bones are soft, his sinews weak,
His grip is nonetheless robust;
Of sexual union unaware,
His organs all completely formed,
His vital force is at its height.
He shouts all day, does not get hoarse:
His person is a harmony.

Harmony experienced is known as constancy;
Constancy experienced is called enlightenment;
Exuberant vitality is ominous, they say;
A bent for vehemence is called aggressiveness.

That things with age decline in strength,
You well may say, suits not the Way;
And not to suit the Way is early death.

PARAPHRASE

The Wise Man is immune to evil. This is due to his childlikeness, which is to say, to the fact that there is complete harmony in his person. No dissipation has wasted his powers.

He shares the constancy of nature and is therefore enlightened. He is not exuberant or aggressive. So may the king be.

If he continues with the Way there will be no decline in his strength or virtue. If he departs from the Way, he is doomed. The last three lines are repeated from Poem 30.

56

Those who know do not talk
And talkers do not know.

Stop your senses,
Close the doors;
Let sharp things be blunted,
Tangles resolved,
The light tempered
And turmoil subdued;
For this is mystic unity
In which the Wise Man is moved
Neither by affection
Nor yet by estrangement
Or profit or loss
Or honor or shame.
Accordingly, by all the world,
He is held highest.

COMMENT

Lines 3–4 copy Poem 52, lines 9–10; while lines 5–8 copy Poem 4, lines 6–9. The general effect of this passage is somewhat extreme and might suggest that the mystic converts the world he lives in into a kind of Hades. This is not the case as other poems illustrate.

Nevertheless, the king must deny himself and be disinterested. As he demonstrates these features of the Wise Man he will be acknowledged the chief of all the world.

57

"Govern the realm by the right,
And battles by stratagem."

The world is won by refraining.
How do I know this is so?
By this:

As taboos increase, people grow poorer;
When weapons abound, the state grows chaotic;
Where skills multiply, novelties flourish;
As statutes increase, more criminals start.

So the Wise Man will say:

As I refrain, the people will reform;
Since I like quiet, they will keep order;
When I forebear, the people will prosper;
When I want nothing, they will be honest.

PARAPHRASE

The government of the realm must be based on justice and righteousness; trickery is for warfare.

The world is to be won by letting it alone; then only will the Way take over. This is indicated by the fact that the more a government acts, the more it has to act. With all our ruling and doing, the world goes badly; it would be better if we were to let it alone altogether. If we did that, the people would be free and, naturally, they would return to the simplicity and honesty of primitive times, to the qualities of the Virginal Block. This is what the king should desire.

58

Listlessly govern:
Happy your people;
Govern exactly:
Restless your people.

"Bad fortune will
Promote the good;
Good fortune, too,
Gives rise to bad."

But who can know to what that leads?
For it is wrong and would assign
To right the strangest derivations
And would mean that goodness
Is produced by magic means!
Has man thus been so long astray?

Accordingly, the Wise Man
Is square but not sharp,
Honest but not malign,
Straight but not severe,
Bright but not dazzling.

COMMENT

The first four lines should be read against the background of Poem 20. "Listless" may refer to Poem 20.

Lines 5–8 are quoted merely for refutation.

In Chinese, to be "square" means to be honest, as in English.

That good fortune begets the bad, and vice versa, comes in for severe attack in this poem, on the ground that it would require magic to make it so. Since everything that happens is governed by the Way, magic is to be ruled out at once. Hence the quoted saying is wrong.

59

"For ruling men or serving God,
There's nothing else like stores saved up."

By "stores saved up" is meant forehandedness,
Accumulated Virtue, such that nothing
Can resist it and its limit
None can guess: such infinite resource
Allows the jurisdiction of the king,
Whose kingdom then will long endure
If it provides the Mother an abode.
Indeed it is the deeply rooted base,
The firm foundation of the Way
To immortality of self and name.

COMMENT

Lines 1–2 are an aphorism quoted to attract attention to the spiritual advice which follows. In line 9, the "Mother" may be a symbol of the Way which accents the female or passive quality of its nature. This is Yinism, as explained in the Introduction, and possibly evidence of the memory of a bygone matriarchy.

60

Rule a large country
As small fish are cooked.

The evil spirits of the world
Lose sanction as divinities
When government proceeds
According to the Way;
But even if they do not lose
Their ghostly countenance and right,
The people take no harm from them;
And if the spirits cannot hurt the folk,
The Wise Man surely does no hurt to them.

Since then the Wise Man and the people
Harm each other not at all,
Their several virtues should converge.

PARAPHRASE

The less you handle small fish when you cook them,
the better. According to the Way, the less you do
about governing people the better your government
will proceed. As the Way comes into its own, the old
superstitions lose their hold: the people take the evil
spirits less seriously.

When it is conceded that the evil spirits can no
longer harm the people, it must appear that at least
the Wise Man is harmless. In which case, the king's
special virtue and the people's virtue should converge
to a common purpose.

61

The great land is a place
To which the streams descend;
It is the concourse and
The female of the world:
Quiescent, underneath,
It overcomes the male.

By quietness and by humility
The great land then puts down the small
And gets it for its own;
But small lands too absorb the great
By their subservience.
Thus some lie low, designing conquest's ends;
While others lowly are, by nature bent
To conquer all the rest.

The great land's foremost need is to increase
The number of its folk;
The small land needs above all else to find
Its folk more room to work.
That both be served and each attain its goal
The great land should attempt humility.

PARAPHRASE

A large land has room for many people and so they
come to it like rivers to the ocean. It is passive, receptive like a woman who first desires and then overcomes a man. Passivity is here proposed as a principle
of international relations.

Beyond passivity, there is humility and this is the
ultimate principle of world dominance. Let the king
consider this well before he embarks on a war.

The psychology of nations great and small is one;

let both be humble and serve each other's need from their respective resources; one has room while the other has people to give. Then there will be peace which always lies at the end of the Way.

62

Like the gods of the shrine in the home,
So the Way and its mystery waits
In the world of material things:
The good man's treasure,
The bad man's refuge.

Fair wordage is ever for sale;
Fair manners are worn like a cloak;
But why should there be such a waste
Of the badness in men?

On the day of the emperor's crowning,
When the three noble dukes are appointed,
Better than chaplets of jade
Drawn by a team of four horses,
Bring the Way as your tribute.

How used the ancients to honor the Way?
Didn't they say that the seeker may find it,
And that sinners who find are forgiven?
So did they lift up the Way and its Virtue
Above everything else in the world.

COMMENT

This is really a poem about the importance of for-
giving sinners. It is a waste to punish bad men. Let
them be forgiven as befits the Wise Man, the king
who does great business on a special day. The Way
requires forgiveness of sin and the Way is truly honored when the sinners are forgiven. Incidentally, the
king's subjects will at once acknowledge that this is
the Way.

63

Act in repose;
Be at rest when you work;
Relish unflavored things.
Great or small,
Frequent or rare,
Requite anger with virtue.

Take hard jobs in hand
While they are easy;
And great affairs too
While they are small.
The troubles of the world
Cannot be solved except
Before they grow too hard.
The business of the world
Cannot be done except
While relatively small.
The Wise Man, then, throughout his life
Does nothing great and yet achieves
A greatness of his own.

Again, a promise lightly made
Inspires little confidence;
Or often trivial, sure that man
Will often come to grief.
Choosing hardship, then, the Wise Man
Never meets with hardship all his life.

PARAPHRASE

The paradox of "acting without doing anything,"
or of simultaneous work and rest, or of relishing the
flavorless, is resolved by the miracle of the Way.

The Wise Man is always serious because he knows

how small troubles grow great and he deals with them while they are easy to handle. The king achieves greatness by choosing hard things before they choose him.

64

A thing that is still is easy to hold.
Given no omen, it is easy to plan.
Soft things are easy to melt.
Small particles scatter easily.
The time to take care is before it is done.
Establish order before confusion sets in.
Tree trunks around which you can reach with
    your arms were at first only minuscule sprouts.
A nine-storied terrace began with a clod.
A thousand-mile journey began with a foot put down.

Doing spoils it, grabbing misses it;
So the Wise Man refrains from doing
    and doesn't spoil anything;
He grabs at nothing and so never misses.

People are constantly spoiling a project when
    it lacks only a step to completion.

To avoid making a mess of it, be as careful of
    the end as you were of the beginning.

So the Wise Man wants the unwanted; he sets no
    high value on anything because it is hard
    to get. He studies what others neglect
    and restores to the world what multitudes
    have passed by. His object is to restore
    everything to its natural course, but he
    dares take no steps to that end.

COMMENT

The king should be firmly grounded in aphorisms.
Here are some of them: they are bits selected from
the popular store of wisdom most agreeable to the
mystics.

65

Those ancients who were skilled in the Way
Did not enlighten people by their rule
But had them ever held in ignorance:
The more the folk know what is going on
The harder it becomes to govern them.

For public knowledge of the government
Is such a thief that it will spoil the realm;
But when good fortune brings good times to all
The land is ruled without publicity.
To know the difference between these two
Involves a standard to be sought and found.

To know that standard always, everywhere,
Is mystic Virtue, justly known as such;
Which Virtue is so deep and reaching far,
It causes a return, things going back
To that prime concord which at first all shared.

PARAPHRASE

Since (1) "there are ways but the Way is uncharted;
there are names but not nature in words," the skilled
governors of ancient times would never pretend to say
what really was going on in the government of the
realm. Any statement would only confuse the people
and make governing them more difficult. A "ministry
of public enlightenment" would be like a plunderer
and spoil everything. When good times are had, it is
because the Way has taken its own free course. The
secret of the Way is not for interested parties or those
who are bound by desire.

The Way is its own standard and producer of good
government on earth. It is the mystic's virtue to know

it and to use it. When it is found and applied, all things will return to that primitive harmony which was once disturbed and, being disturbed, gave rise to mankind's ineluctable problems.

66

How could the rivers and the seas
Become like kings to valleys?
Because of skill in lowliness
They have become the valley's lords.

So then to be above the folk,
You speak as if you were beneath;
And if you wish to be out front,
Then act as if you were behind.

The Wise Man so is up above
But is no burden to the folk;
His station is ahead of them
To see they do not come to harm.

The world will gladly help along
The Wise Man and will bear no grudge.
Since he contends not for his own
The world will not contend with him.

PARAPHRASE

The king can attain his true character as a king only
by humility and disinterestedness, both of which virtues must be real and apparent.

67

Everywhere, they say the Way, our doctrine,
Is so very like detested folly;
But greatness of its own alone explains
Why it should be thus held beyond the pale.
If it were only orthodox, long since
It would have seemed a small and petty thing!

I have to keep three treasures well secured:
The first, compassion; next, frugality;
And third, I say that never would I once
Presume that I should be the whole world's chief.

Given compassion, I can take courage;
Given frugality, I can abound;
If I can be the world's most humble man,
Then I can be its highest instrument.

Bravery today knows no compassion;
Abundance is, without frugality,
And eminence without humility:
This is the death indeed of all our hope.

In battle, 'tis compassion wins the day;
Defending, 'tis compassion that is firm:
Compassion arms the people God would save!

PARAPHRASE

The doctrine of the Way has been generally attacked, presumably by orthodox Confucianists, as heterodox, "detestable folly." It has not been understood by people satisfied with a petty orthodoxy. Presumably the king will understand so great a doctrine where others have failed.

The failure to understand it is moral rather than intellectual. Compassion, frugality and humility: these three great virtues are absent from political life. Their absence can be fatal to the nation. It is, however, chiefly compassion that connects the people to the will of God.

68

A skillful soldier is not violent;
An able fighter does not rage;
A mighty conqueror does not give battle;
A great commander is a humble man.

You may call this pacific virtue;
Or say that it is mastery of men;
Or that it is rising to the measure of God,
Or to the stature of the ancients.

PARAPHRASE

The man of the Way is no doctrinaire pacifist; he may be a soldier, a fighter, a conqueror, or one who commands and is obeyed. He is not, however, a man of violence; the imponderables are the essence of his art. Let the king take note.

This view leads to peace, and as the king is able to keep peace with honor, he rises to God's measure or compares favorably with the worthies of ancient times who followed the Way.

69

The strategists have a saying:
>   "If I cannot be host,
>   Then let me be guest.
>   But if I dare not advance
>   Even an inch,
>   Then let me retire a foot."

This is what they call
>   A campaign without a march,
>   Sleeves up but no bare arms,
>   Shooting but no enemies,
>   Or arming without weapons.

Than helpless enemies, nothing is worse:
To them I lose my treasures.
When opposing enemies meet,
The compassionate man is the winner!

PARAPHRASE

The strategists are absurd. Little bankrupt feudal states, like sleeves with no arms in them, marching and going nowhere, arming without weapons, plotting moves and countermoves as the empire sinks into chaos, each hoping to conquer the rest: this is the picture the king must contemplate.

Actually, he must have realized that nothing could be worse for him than that all the little states around his should be helpless before his attack. He would then succumb to temptation and his three treasures (see Poem 67) would be lost. It is the one who loses the war that really wins it!

Comment: The first saying quoted above means: if I cannot take care of an enemy on my own ground, let me invade his.

70

My words are easy just to understand:
To live by them is very easy too;
Yet it appears that none in all the world
Can understand or make them come to life.

My words have ancestors, my works a prince;
Since none know this, unknown I too remain.
But honor comes to me when least I'm known:
The Wise Man, with a jewel in his breast,
Goes clad in garments made of shoddy stuff.

PARAPHRASE

"My yoke is easy and my burden light"; yet it is
very hard for people to take it up.

Words, precepts and doctrines, like people, must
have pedigrees and high authority to gain respect and
fame. Mine have precedents and principle but this
does not get them recognition and so I too am ig-
nored. In this respect, at least, I share the honors of
all those prophets who have borne priceless truth in
their hearts but have looked like beggars all their lives.
It would be better for all concerned if the king had a
jewel in his breast. The shoddy clothes could be
optional.

71

To know that you are ignorant is best;
To know what you do not, is a disease;
But if you recognize the malady
Of mind for what it is, then that is health.

The Wise Man has indeed a healthy mind;
He sees an aberration as it is
And for that reason never will be ill.

COMMENT

Socrates in Greece, perhaps a century before the
writer of this poem, developed its observation as irony
and moral duty: here it is seen that the knowledge of
one's real ignorance is indispensable to mental health.
No one is in danger, says the writer, so long as he can
be critical of his own mental states. The king should
develop this power.

72

If people do not dread your majesty,
A greater dread will yet descend on them.
See then you do not cramp their dwelling place,
Or immolate their children or their stock,
Nor anger them by your own angry ways.

It is the Wise Man's way to know himself,
And never to reveal his inward thoughts;
He loves himself but so, is not set up;
He chooses this in preference to that.

PARAPHRASE

When people no longer stand in awe of their king,
divine wrath, much more dreadful, will overtake them.
So the king will do well not to imprison them or oppress them in their homes. He should not take revenge
by killing their children or confiscating their livestock.
He must not make them resentful by his resentment
of them.

According to Poem 71, the king should know his
own attitudes and impulses for what they are, but he
should never show them to the people. Let him respect himself but not be conceited. Then he can be
discriminating in the proper sense of the word, choosing benevolence and rejecting compulsive force.

73

A brave man who dares to, will kill;
A brave man who dares not, spares life;
And from them both come good and ill.
"God hates some folks, but who knows why?"
The Wise Man hesitates there too:
God's Way is bound to conquer all
But not by strife does it proceed.

Not by words does God get answers:
He calls them not and all things come.
Master plans unfold but slowly,
Like God's wide net enclosing all:
Its mesh is coarse but none are lost.

PARAPHRASE

It also takes brave men to dare not to kill others,
when the king wants killing done. Perhaps the king is
as well served by one as the other. Who knows what
part God plays in war or punishment? The king must
hesitate before he puts himself in place of God. All
one knows is that God's will is done and that his will
is not strife.

God gets what he wants in his own way, the Way;
he does not issue words, but his master plan is to be
seen unfolding like a great net which encloses all and
from which not one escapes.

74

The people do not fear at all to die;
What's gained therefore by threat'ning them with death?
If you could always make them fear decease,
As if it were a strange event and rare,
Who then would dare to take and slaughter them?
The executioner is always set
To slay, but those who substitute for him
Are like the would-be master carpenters
Who try to chop as that skilled craftsman does
And nearly always mangle their own hands!

PARAPHRASE

Capital punishment is no deterrent to crime because death is commonplace and people do not fear it. If, however, the king goes in for mass executions to the extent that they become remarkable, he will need many soldiers, who are, in effect, executioners. Who would dare to be candidates for this job when it might lead to their own execution, as frequently, in such cases, it does?

75

The people starve because of those
Above them, who consume by tax
In grain and kind more than their right.
For this, the people are in want.

The people are so hard to rule
Because of those who are above them,
Whose interference makes distress.
For this, they are so hard to rule.

The people do not fear to die;
They too demand to live secure:
For this, they do not fear to die.
So they, without the means to live,
In virtue rise above those men
Who value life above its worth.

PARAPHRASE

In the last century but one before the end of the
Chou dynasty, the ruling classes of China are demoral-
ized. They feel frightened at the prospect of growing
disorder. They attempt to secure themselves at the
expense of the people.

The people, who are familiar with death, are not
intimidated by it. Their will to live is greater than their
fear of death. In this, they are superior to the nobility
whose fear of death is greater than their will to live.

76

Alive, a man is supple, soft;
In death, unbending, rigorous.
All creatures, grass and trees, alive
Are plastic but are pliant too,
And dead, are friable and dry.

Unbending rigor is the mate of death,
And yielding softness, company of life:
Unbending soldiers get no victories;
The stiffest tree is readiest for the axe.
The strong and mighty topple from their place;
The soft and yielding rise above them all.

PARAPHRASE

Contrary to tradition, the female principle, as softness and pliableness, is to be associated with life and
survival. Because he can yield, a man can survive. In
contrast, the male principle, which is here assumed to
be rigorous and hard, makes a man break under pres-
sure. At any rate, the last two lines make a fair and
oft-told description of revolution as many generations
of people have seen it.

77

Is not God's Way much like a bow well bent?
The upper part has been disturbed, pressed down;
The lower part is raised up from its place;
The slack is taken up; the slender width
Is broader drawn; for thus the Way of God
Cuts people down when they have had too much,
And fills the bowls of those who are in want.
But not the way of man will work like this:
The people who have not enough are spoiled
For tribute to the rich and surfeited.

Who can benefit the world
From stored abundance of his own?
He alone who has the Way,
The Wise Man who can act apart
And not depend on others' whims;
But not because of his high rank
Will he succeed; he does not wish
To flaunt superiority.

PARAPHRASE

God's Way is to "put down the mighty from their seats" and to exalt "them of low degree." "He hath filled the hungry with good things; and the rich he hath sent empty away." But this is not the way of men, who rob the poor for the rich.

So there is nothing to be hoped for from the rich; only the Wise Man, the king, who is on the Way and has its virtue, can hope to put justice to work in society. Only he is independent enough to succeed in the effort and only he has sufficient humility to try.

78

Nothing is weaker than water,
But when it attacks something hard
Or resistant, then nothing withstands it,
And nothing will alter its way.

Everyone knows this, that weakness prevails
Over strength and that gentleness conquers
The adamant hindrance of men, but that
Nobody demonstrates how it is so.

Because of this the Wise Man says
That only one who bears the nation's shame
Is fit to be its hallowed lord;
That only one who takes upon himself
The evils of the world may be its king.

This is paradox.

PARAPHRASE

The analogy of the irresistible power of water is
stated again, as in Poem 43. The paradox of weakness
overcoming strength is well known in theory but no
one seems to be able to make it work.

This leads to a thought of the king. He must be
able to make it work if he is fit for his high office, as
"lord of the altars of the soil and the grain." Only as
the king is able to take upon himself the sins of the
world can he be king. This is the paradox of the power
of nonresistance, the accomplishment of those who,
of themselves, do nothing but who allow the Way to
use them.

79

How can you think it is good
To settle a grievance too great
To ignore, when the settlement
Surely evokes other piques?

The Wise Man therefore will select
The left-hand part of contract tallies:
He will not put the debt on other men.
This virtuous man promotes agreement;
The vicious man allots the blame.

"Impartial though the Way of God may be,
It always favors good men."

PARAPHRASE

To settle a major cause of discontent so that other grievances are bound to ensue is poor administration.

Contracts are made by lines cut on bamboo tally slips which are then split in two. The debtor, being considered the inferior, gets the left-hand portion. To show his humility, the Wise Man deliberately chooses the inferior section, assumes the guilt or the debt, and thus disarms the adversary. This is the way of the man of virtue. The vicious man, by contrast, tries to fix the blame or debt on others.

God's Way is no respecter of persons but when a man is good, the Way is on his side.

80

The ideal land is small
Its people very few,
Where tools abound
Ten times or yet
A hundredfold
Beyond their use;
Where people die
And die again
But never emigrate;
Have boats and carts
Which no one rides.
Weapons have they
And armor too,
But none displayed.
The folk returns
To use again
The knotted cords.
Their meat is sweet;
Their clothes adorned,
Their homes at peace,
Their customs charm.

And neighbor lands
Are juxtaposed
So each may hear
The barking dogs,
The crowing cocks
Across the way;
Where folks grow old
And folks will die
And never once
Exchange a call.

COMMENT

This describes the ideal commonwealth, the land of
no-place (Utopia), quite in contrast to the almost contemporary *Republic* of Plato.

The knotted cords, a means of memorandum, preceded the invention of writing in China, as in other lands. The Chinese abacus is descended from knotted cords but has sliding knots.

81

As honest words may not sound fine,
Fine words may not be honest ones;
A good man does not argue, and
An arguer may not be good!
The knowers are not learnéd men
And learnéd men may never know.

The Wise Man does not hoard his things;
Hard-pressed, from serving other men,
He has enough and some to spare;
But having given all he had,
He then is very rich indeed.

God's Way is gain that works no harm;
The Wise Man's way, to do his work
Without contending for a crown.

COMMENT

In the last stanza, the king is advised to work according to God's Way, without considering his crown,
i.e., let him not consider the demands of politicians
and sycophants but hew to the line that meets the
specifications of the Way.

Afterword

The *Daode jing* [*Tao Té Ching*] or *Laozi* [*Lao Tzu*] is the most "translated" work in the world after the Bible.* About eight hundred versions into European languages have appeared—about half into English. "Translated" is placed within quotes because most are not strictly translations but rather rewordings based on earlier learned translations. These tend to be interpretive paraphrases by those who cannot read the original and often depart greatly from the literal meaning.

What passes for "translations" of the *Laozi* include a range of approaches: (1) Scholarly translation, word for word, critically edited, arrived at with philological expertise and attention to its literary, philosophical/religious, and historical contexts, aimed at recovering the original meaning and intent of the text. (2) Scholarly translation with added explanatory material—usually a mixture of references (sometimes unacknowledged) to Chinese commentaries and the translator's own interpretations. (3) A combination of the first and second approaches that presents both the integral translation of an early Chinese commentary and a new translation of the classic text interpreted in light of the commentary.† (4) Literary paraphrase of the original text by

Pinyin, the official romanization system established in China to transcribe Chinese characters, is now almost universally used in Western scholarly writings about China and so is used here. Blakney used the Wade-Giles system, the scholarly norm of his day, so to ease the reader from the one to the other, at each first instance of transcription, I give the name or term in *pinyin* and then provide a Wade-Giles transcription in brackets—provided it appears somewhere in the body of Blakney's text. Hereafter the title of the Daoist [Taoist] classic will be given as *Laozi* and *Tao* as *Dao.*
†See Richard John Lynn, *The Classic of the Way and Virtue: A New Translation of the Tao-te ching of Laozi as Interpreted by Wang Bi* (New York: Columbia University Press, 1999).

translators into more accessible English. Such versions largely try to preserve something of the literal meaning but readily sacrifice it to achieve increased readability and clarity. (5) Subjective interpretation of the text, often based on nontraditional Chinese traditions or habits of thought, usually by those who cannot read the original—and often think it unnecessary to do so. Such versions exploit the work of one or more of the first four kinds of translation. The vast majority of "translations" of the *Laozi* are found here—caveat emptor!

Combinations of the first four approaches often occur, and Blakney's version, while combining elements from the first and second, belongs mostly to the fourth. He should not be assigned to the fifth because he was acquainted with Chinese ways of reading the text and refrains from imposing a foreign reading on it. Although his interpretation draws on acquaintance with Western mysticism, this is not incompatible with Chinese mystical readings, and though a devout Christian and Congregational minister and missionary, he does not interpret it from any sectarian Christian perspective. The Introduction includes a detailed account of the literary, philosophical/religious, and historical contexts. Although all this can be improved on thanks to more than fifty years of scholarly advance, it still is generally accurate and reads well. However, Blakney makes no attempt to confront the many philological problems besetting the text but instead accepts as stands a modern edition of the text as printed in *Lao jie lao* [*Lao Chieh Lao*] (Let the *Laozi* Explain the *Laozi*) (Preface, 11), published together with a concordance by Cai Tinggan (1861–1935) in 1922. Cai explains the meaning of the title in the *fanli* (Principles of Compilation) and also states that the text is taken from the *Wuyingdian juzhenban congshu* (Collectanea of Selected Rare Editions Printed in the Palace of Martial Heroism [Imperial Printing Press and Bindery]) (1774–94) and published separately in 1900. This reproduces the so-called Wang Bi (226–49) recension, so called because Wang's commentary is associated with it.

However, modern scholarship proves that this is *not* the text Wang actually commented on, since it obviously refers occasionally to different wordings of the *Laozi*. Such textual variants have plagued its study for centuries (five other recensions exist, all with significant variants), a situation further complicated by modern archaeological discoveries: (1) Two transcriptions on silk were found in 1973 in a tomb closed in 168 B.C. at Mawangdui (Hunan). The first can be dated to before 206 B.C. and the second to 206–194 B.C. Each differs in places from the other as well as from any of the recensions. (2) Three bamboo-slip texts corresponding to parts of the *Laozi* were found in 1993 in a tomb dated to the mid-fourth to the early third centuries B.C. at Guodian (Hubei). These texts follow a different sequence and also often differ in wording from the recensions. However, none of this would have interested Blakney, who was primarily concerned with the text as a book of wisdom—a scripture of mystical insight. Nevertheless, Blakney both recognized that the author of the *Laozi* was legendary (Introduction, 32) and realized that no single person authored the text but that it was a collection edited by an "established but informal cult" (Introduction, 48)—an astute observation with which recent scholarship agrees. This is why the text is now usually referred to as "the *Laozi*" and not by "Laozi."

Philology aside, Blakney demonstrates competence in reading the original. Although he calls the eighty-one passages "poems," the great majority are actually short prose pieces (the Chinese never classified the *Laozi* as poetry, despite the fact that some parts rhyme). Other translators refer to them as "chapters," but because of their short length, this seems misleading. I prefer "sections." Blakney turns all these sections into unrhymed English verse in various meters, but these literary paraphrases should not be confused with the "Paraphrase" that follows each, for they are his own interpretations of the translated sections. As such, they are prose paraphrases of his literary paraphrases. The "Paraphrase" is sometimes followed by a "Comment," which supplies additional information and further explanation. Despite paraphrasing throughout, his grasp of both syntax and vocabulary must have been good, for it allowed him to stay close enough to the original meaning so that when his English is compared with the original the correspondences are readily apparent, though these are sometimes quite tenuous and tend even more to interpretive paraphrase. Moreover, since Blakney is familiar with the cultural context, he often comes up with phraseology that captures connotations that transcend literal expression. Nevertheless, we have to keep in mind that Blakney deliberately paraphrased and readily discarded original syntax to rewrite lines to read fluently in English and substituted familiar English diction for what he considered obscure wording of the original. Regarding translation and interpretation, he wrote:

> I cannot pretend to see the world as Chinese of the third to the sixth century before Christ saw it, and I do not believe that any amount of scientific sifting of the facts would enable a person of this century to do so. There will always be a semantic gulf between them and us, one that must be bridged by adding insight and imagination to considered evidence. . . . It is my belief that a finished translation should be free of all traces of the original language, especially when they mar English diction. (Preface, 10)

Few if any learned translators of the *Laozi*—or any Chinese text in archaic or classical Chinese—would now agree with him. Although it's probably impossible ever to get such texts "exactly right," progress during the last half century in the systematic historical and philological study of ancient Chinese texts has brought us notably closer to getting them right, and the best of our translators are producing versions that much more accurately capture original meaning. The "semantic gulf" is now being bridged not just by "insight and imagination" but by utilizing recent advances in lexicography and understanding of archaic and classical Chinese grammar, not just in the West but more important in philological resources developed in China. Modern scholarship on ancient Chinese thought—as with all premodern fields—has burgeoned in China during the past twenty-five years (longer in Taiwan, Singapore, and Hong Kong) and annotated translation into modern Chinese of the *Laozi* and other early texts has steadily increased in quantity and quality. Moreover, Japanese scholarship on China continues to provide a wide range of valuable reference and research materials as well as many excellent translations of Chinese classics into modern Japanese. We thus have access to research and translation resources—including those available on the Internet in all pertinent languages—that Blakney could not have dreamed of in his day.

His contention that translation "should be free of all traces of the original language" is not so easily addressed. Like many contemporary translators, I try to find syntactic equivalents that correspond to the grammatical elements of archaic and classical Chinese and accurately reproduce the idiom of the original while not "marring English diction." For example, Blakney's version of Section 14 (concerning qualities of the elusive Dao) begins:

> They call it elusive, and say
> That one looks
> But it never appears.
> They say that indeed it is rare,
> Since one listens,
> But never a sound.
> Subtle, they call it, and say
> That one grasps it
> But never gets hold.
> These three complaints amount
> To only one, which is
> Beyond all resolution.
> (*Tao Té Ching*, 74)

By contrast, I try to keep the Chinese word order and same parts of speech, leave nothing out, and add only words that though not explicitly there are yet present by implication, reproduce the syntactic structure of the discourse, and ensure the best match between original and English choice of words, aided by the glosses of Wang Bi's commentary:

> When we look for it but see it not, we call it the invisible. When we listen for it but hear it not, we call it the inaudible. When we try to touch it but find it not, we call it the imperceptible. Since these three aspects of it are impossible to probe, it remains a single amorphous unity.*

The two versions are not all that different, but we can examine Blakney's rendering of the last complex sentence, *ci sanzhe buke zhijie, gu hun er wei yi*, as "These three complaints amount/To only one, which is/Beyond all resolution." *Ci sanzhe* "these three aspects," or simply "these three," *yi* "the invisible," *xi* "the inaudible," and *wei* "the imperceptible" (Blakney's "elusive," "rare," and "subtle") are not "complaints," for *zhijie* is not a noun but a verbal compound, "to probe," and while *jie* alone can mean "complain/complaint," this ignores the *zhi*, which is integral to the meaning. Moreover, "complain/complaint" is a secondary meaning— the primary meaning is "investigate," "interrogate," "probe."† Blakney also disregards the *buke* "impossible to," perhaps because it does not fit the paraphrase he had in mind. "Amounts to only one, which is beyond all resolution" is actually rather good, though still a paraphrase; my "it remains a single amorphous entity" is also a paraphrase. A more literal rendering would be "since these three cannot be probed, we lump them

---

*Richard John Lynn, *The Classic of the Way and Virtue*, 72.
†Luo Zhufeng, ed., *Hanyu dacidian* (Great Dictionary of the Chinese Language), 8:795, where this very passage in the *Laozi* is cited as illustration for the definition of *zhijie*. The entry on *jie* is 11:156.

together as one." I now suspect that *zhijie* is a term borrowed from forensics and used metaphorically here: as if three suspects were interrogated for a crime and since it was impossible to prove the respective degrees of culpability, all were lumped together as equally culpable and punished as one—a subtle example of humor meant to show how ridiculous it is to try to identify or define the Dao.

One can find other such places that warrant improvement, but overall Blakney's translation is accurate enough to deserve new reading. However, the work's greatest value lies in the observations made both in his "Paraphrases" and "Comments" and his reflections on Chinese and Western mysticism in the Introduction. His "Key Concepts" are especially rich in comparative insight and seem as meaningful today as they did fifty years ago. These are aspects of Blakney's work that were most favorably commented on when it first appeared, for example:

> . . . the judgment of the quality of the translation, as well as the interpretation, lie upon the immediate intuition obtained through self-cultivation by the writer on his own, to match that of the original author of the classic. . . . Through his long years of devotion and contemplation on the teachings of the *Tao Té Ching* and because of his own intuitive knowledge of religious mysticism he is certainly equipped with an "acquaintance" with what is ultimate reality, *Tao*, "all-embracing" and yet nameless, indescribable, beyond telling.*

> Blakney studied the book for thirty years and obviously lived according to its teachings. . . . His version deserves the attention of those who want to grapple with the confusing and distressing complexities of life which are often not essentially different from those

so whimsically viewed by The Old One in Central China so long, long ago.*

But we have to ask, how did a devout Yankee Congregational churchman become so involved with the *Laozi*? Equally important, how did he acquire the linguistic expertise and cultural familiarity to produce such a study and translation of it? The story of his life tells us the answer to both questions.

Although the saying "may you live in interesting times" is often identified as "an ancient Chinese saying," no evidence exists for a Chinese origin (it probably originated in America during the 1950s). Nevertheless, Raymond Bernard Blakney (1895–1970) was so cursed—or blessed—depending on the point of view, for he led a cosmopolitan life rich in experience during a time of great turmoil and conflict.† Earning a civil engineering degree at MIT and also graduating from Boston University School of Theology just as America entered World War I, he was ordained and served as an army chaplain during 1918. It was then that he met Laura Marsh, an army nurse, who soon became his wife. They set off to China in 1920, first to Peking, or as it was then called Peiping (Beiping), "Northern Peace," where Blakney began the study of Chinese, and then a

*William Hung [Hong Ye], endorsement for R. B. Blakney, *The Way of Life: A New Translation of The Tao Té Ching* (New York: New American Library, 1955), Frontpiece: "Chinese Mysticism."

†Michael Fales, Director of Church Relations and Campus Ministries, Olivet College, started me down the right path to the facts of Blakney's life, and Art Stevens, Former Professor of Political Science, Olivet College and a close friend of Blakney's, supplied a broad account of Blakney's career and a description of his character and personal interests. I am also grateful to Tom Kitt, who maintains a Web site devoted to self-realization and spirituality, "One Positive" at http://onepositive.com, for drawing my attention to William Hung's endorsement of Blakney's *Laozi* book. Charles Blakney, Congregational minister and misssionary now retired in South Hadley, Massachusetts, gave a detailed account of his father's life, without which the following biography could not have been written.

few years later to Fuzhou (Foochow), where he served until 1928 as professor of mathematical physics at Fukien Christian University. An enthusiastic language student, he even published a work on the subject: *A Course in the Analysis of Chinese Characters*, Chinese title *Hanzi yanjiu* (Shanghai: The Commercial Press, 1926; reprint 1935), an etymological dictionary of Chinese characters that for a time was widely used in the field but now has long been superseded by more rigorous and comprehensive works. Two children were born in China—Robert in Peking (1920) and Jean in Fuzhou (1922).

It was probably in Peking that Blakney became acquainted with William Hung, who wrote the sympathetic critique of Blakney's *Laozi* book quoted above. Hung, just two years Blakney's senior, taught history and religion courses at Yenching University (1923–24) and was Dean of the College of Arts and Sciences (1924–27). Hung shared Blakney's Christian faith and had a large circle of friends in the Western community. Hung was a Mason and member of the Peking Rotary Club; his popularity even extended to his being elected president of the American College Club.*

However, by the end of the 1920s and on the eve of the Great Depression, American funds to support education in China dried up, so the Blakneys had to return to the United States. After a brief stint selling encyclopedias door-to-door, Blakney became minister of the North Parish Congregational Church in Sanford, Maine, where the Blakneys' third child, Charles, was born (1928). Five years later Blakney was called to the First Congregational Church in Williamstown, Massachusetts, in the middle of Williams College, where aside from parish duties he coached the college debating team. While in Williamstown, he turned from Chinese to study Middle High German and produced *Meister Eckhart, A Modern Translation* (New York & London:

*Egan, Susan Chan, *A Latterday Confucian: Reminiscences of William Hung (1893–1980)* (Harvard University Press, 1987), 90, 99–110.

Harper, 1941; seventh edition 2004), which translates and comments on the works of the medieval mystic Johannes Eckhart (1260–1328). The contents include such sections as "The Influence of Meister Eckhart," "Mysticism of Two Kinds," "The Background in 1300," "Eckhart's Life and Work," "Some Source Ideas," "Meister Eckhart's Talks of Instruction," and "Sermons." For this work Blakney was awarded an honorary doctorate by Williams College in 1946, when he returned to Williamstown after army service during World War II.

In format and general approach, *Meister Eckhart* served as model for the *The Way of Life: A New Translation of the Tao Té Ching* (first edition 1955), which locates the text in both historical and literary contexts and examines its significance for ancient Chinese thought, comparing it to that of Confucius and Mencius, Mozi, legalism, and yin-yang theory. Although instead of "Some Source Ideas" as in *Meister Eckhart*, Blakney analyzes "Key Concepts," the methodology is the same, and his "Paraphrase" and "Comment" on the text also resemble his approach in *Meister Eckhart*. However, the major commonality of the two is his personal identification with the basic purpose, as he saw it, underlying both texts: "The mystic's passion is satisfied only with the sense of Ultimate reality, the God, Godhead or God-ness that is back of the world of mind and nature. . . . Reality, howsoever designated, is One; it is an all-embracing unity from which nothing can be separated." Blakney follows this characterization with a quote from the writings of Meister Eckhart: "So I say that likeness born of the One, leads the soul to God, for he is One, unbegotten unity. . . ." (Introduction, 33).

In 1943, Blakney took leave from his parish in Williamstown to rejoin the Army Chaplain Corps and taught for a year at the US Army Chaplain School, then located at Harvard University. In 1944 he was sent to England to serve as a Sector Chaplain, and after D-Day, he was in France, where he became acquainted with General Henry Aurand, soon to be transferred to

Kunming as Commanding General of Services of Supply, China Theatre. Aurand wanted to take Blakney with him because he spoke Chinese, but as a captain, Blakney was not eligible for such transfer, so Aurand had him transferred into Services of Supply and promoted him to major. After arrival in Kunming, Aurand then had him transferred back into the Chaplain Corps, a move that General Eisenhower himself, according to Ike's memoirs, followed with amused approval. Blakney also served as a translator and adviser to Aurand's staff until the end of hostilities.

After a short time in Williamstown, the Blakneys returned to China in 1946, this time to Peking, where he did translations for the United Church Board for World Ministries, resulting in *The Life and Teachings of Jesus*, coauthored by Zi Zhong, a Chinese convert, *The Life and Teachings of Paul*, coauthored by Elmer Galt (1883–1964), a Congregational missionary, and *Selections from the Old Testament*, coauthored by Peng Jinzhang, a writer of Christian tracts in Chinese, and *Some Fell into Good Ground: Sermons Preached in the Congregational Churches of North China 1947–1948*, also coauthored by Peng Jinzhang—all published in bilingual editions, with English and Chinese on facing pages, by the Li Min Press in Peiping during 1947 and 1948. When it seemed inevitable that the People's Liberation Army would soon occupy Peiping late in 1948 (shortly afterward renamed Beijing, "Northern Capital" because it became the capital of China again), the Blakneys departed China for good, spending a year first in the Philippines as missionaries, and then back to the United States, where Raymond Blakney became President of Olivet College (1950–57), a liberal arts institution in Michigan founded by Congregational churchmen in 1844, on the principles of coeducation, social responsibility, and abolitionism. It was then that Blakney produced his work on the *Laozi*, which he had begun to study thirty years earlier in Fuzhou.

In 1957 the Blakneys moved to Athens, where he became President of the American College of Greece

(Pierce College), administered by the United Church Board for World Ministries. He was in Athens for three years, during which he completed his last publication, *An Immanuel Kant Reader* (New York: Harper, 1960). Blakney found Kant (1724–1804) a congenial thinker, especially for his nonsectarianism, his assertion that practical necessity underlies a belief in God, an idea developed in his *Critique of Pure Reason*, and for his argument from morality for the existence of God—from the demands of moral duty, the "categorical imperative." Blakney devoted all his life to moral duty and being a seeker of religious truth; his work on Kant reflects both tendencies. In his later years, he seems to have become increasingly attracted to Kant's careful reasoning, in contrast to his earlier fascination with Eastern and Western mysticism, which rely so much on poetry and mythic imagery for expression.

After retirement, Blakney served as an interim minister, first in Arizona and later in Seattle. His last years were spent at Pilgrim Place in Claremont, California, a Christian ecumenical retirement community near the Claremont Colleges—surely an important attraction for such a scholar and thinker. Blakney died suddenly while walking home one day after working in one of the college libraries.

—Richard John Lynn
Professor Emeritus of Chinese
Thought and Literature
University of Toronto

Signet Classics

IDEAS THAT HAVE CHANGED THE WAY WE THINK ABOUT THE WORLD

GREAT DIALOGUES OF PLATO (*Revised Edition*) PLATO

The complete texts of *The Republic, The Apology, Crito, Phaedo, Ion, Meno, Euthydemus,* and *Symposium* in W.H.D. Rouse's widely-acclaimed translation. Through the writings of Plato, Socrates, Greece's greatest philosopher, can centuries later still teach us how to think.

THE ORIGIN OF SPECIES CHARLES DARWIN

The famous classic on evolution that exploded into public controversy and revolutionized the course of science. Next to *The Bible* no work has been quite as influential—and none more controversial—in virtually every aspect of human thought.

Available wherever books are sold or at
signetclassics.com

S329

READ THE TOP 20
SIGNET CLASSICS